THE GREAT PORT

A Passage through New York

THE
GREAT
PORT

A Passage through New York

JAN MORRIS

With photographs by Albert Belva

OXFORD UNIVERSITY PRESS

NEW YORK

Library of Congress Cataloging in Publication Data

Morris, Jan, 1926-

The great port.

Reprint. Originally published: New York: Harcourt,

Brace & World, 1969.

Bibliography: p.

1. New York (N.Y.)—Harbor.

2. New York (N.Y.)—Description.

I. Title.

HE554.N7M63   1985   387.1'09747'1   85-336

ISBN 0-19-503576-3 (pbk.)

Printing (last digit): 9 8 7 6 5 4 3 2 1

Printed in the United States of America

For

AUSTIN TOBIN

a scrimshaw souvenir

of his Leviathan

The universal will to move
—to move, move, move, as
an end in itself, an appetite
at any price . . .

HENRY JAMES
The American Scene

RESERVATIONS

This navigation through New York, as the least persistent reader will soon discover (for it comes on page 5) was commissioned out of the blue by the Port of New York Authority: but beyond correcting factual errors, and making a few diffident gestures of self-defense, the Authority's executives did not interfere with the substance of the book. For better or for worse, it is all mine.

Was all mine, anyway, for this reprint appears more than 15 years after the work's original publication, and both the Port of New York and I have moved on since then. I have more or less shifted my identity: the port has shifted its functions and its shape, adapting to new patterns of trade, new geographical groupings, and new techniques of transportation.

However when I read through the book to prepare this new edition I did not find it exactly out of date. If it is a period piece in some ways, through no merit of its own it is timeless in others, and though I felt obliged to fiddle here and there with the detail, I left the whole untouched. For New York, on the surface the most volatile and kaleidoscopic of cities, is in essence, I think, peculiarly permanent. Contrary to the popular view, in fundamentals it really changes very little down the generations.

It remains now, as it was in 1969, as it was indeed in 1669, above all a landing-stage, a conduit, a place of movement, and its character is governed always by the successive tides of energy that flood perpetually through it. Not just fissile things, but peoples, ideas, philosophies—these are and always have been the prime commodities of the port of New York, and the city's *raisons d'êtres.*

Since I wrote *The Great Port* the transatlantic liner trade has almost ended and the maritime business of New York has been dispersed more widely around the bay. The New York skyline has been ineradicably altered by the building of the two World Trade Center towers in lower Manhattan, and sundry lesser skyscrapers elsewhere. The social pattern of the place has continued its endless mazy motion, as different kinds of residents, of different incomes, of different race, migrate here and there among the zip-codes and the boroughs, obeying immemorial laws of self-advancement or fraternity.

But the same winds blow out of the sea as blow through the closing lines of my book; the Sandy Hook pilots sailed out this very morning, as they sail through my Chapter 8, to guide another few ships through the Narrows; the distant bridges may still be glimpsed, as their builder glimpses them through his telescope on page 151, from the upper floors of the Carlyle; the aircraft are often jammed nose to tail, as Mr. Belva's picture shows them, on the runways of JFK; and now as then, the presence of the great haven can still send a frisson down my spine, when I see it standing there, so beautiful, so terrible, so squalid and so magnificent, veiled in its own mist, lit by its own steely radiance upon the Atlantic foreshore.

CONTENTS

Photographs between pp. 50 and 51, 114 and 115, 178 and 179.

One

PHYSICAL

Chapter 1

THE PASSAGE BOOKED

Mr. Austin J. Tobin ate sparingly, I thought, but I was hungry, for I had driven down from North Wales to meet him. This gave him a chance to elaborate his message, and me an opportunity to sum him up. He was not how I imagined a New York harbor man. He was a small solid lawyer, weathered but cherubic, like an American Buddha. His voice was gentle but there was a steeliness to his eye, imperfectly disguised in humor. I had been told that he was one of the highest-paid public servants in the United States, and one of the most powerful men in New York, and it seemed to me that while he would be a mellow and witty dinner host, he might be an awkward opponent to handle, face to face across a conference table with any flaming issue in between.

His conversation was pitched low. He even rambled rather. My own conception of the port of New York was cast in a romantic-historical *genre*. I saw it peopled by swaggering Yankee merchants and schooner captains, and colored by flying clippers from the East. I imagined it flavored with bootleg mayhem and Brooklynese, and ornamented by Myrna Loys and Betty Grables, crossing their

silken legs before trilby-hatted newsreel men on the promenade decks of Atlantic Greyhounds. High-bridged toffee-
nosed tugs crossed my line of surmise, too, and ferryboats
puffed towards dingy New Jersey destinations with aboriginal
names, and steam trains clanked across immense latticed
bridges, and Harbor Precinct police patrolled set-jawed
through ominous creeks. I imagined it mainly in the past
tense, for during my own visits to New York I had seldom
thought of the city as a port at all: from high skyscraper
rooms in mid-Manhattan I might sometimes glimpse a liner
sidling behind the apartment blocks, but the waterfront and
its life seemed only incidental, or marginal, to the affairs of
the city. For me New York was a harbor of history—of the
privateers and the great sailing ships, of the Blue Riband of
the Atlantic, of Ellis Island, of the wartime troopships and
the packet boats.

Mr. Tobin's port sounded something else. At first my
attention was on my lamb chop, but as he talked I began
to feel obscurely excited by his company. He was like a
messenger from some distant powerhouse. He seemed to
bring the heat with him, insulated in courtesy. He talked
about turmoil, experiment, bitter rivalry, tragedy. He told
me of glorious bridges and colossal tunnels and desperately
expanding airports. He said they were at that moment
erecting the two tallest buildings on earth. He spoke of
political passions, crosscurrents of interest and morality, grand
ocean views, helicopters, new kinds of ship, new kinds of
aircraft, terrible problems of congestion and racial distrust
and metropolitan poverty. He talked, above all, of a city—
in a sense The City—whose basic purpose was movement:
a funnel, channel, or duct, around whose wharves and
waterways had arisen the most spectacular of all human
agglomerations—its *raison d'être* the coming and going of
everything, its job in history portage.

"Would it interest you to write a book about it all?" Mr. Tobin mildly inquired. "We would be delighted to give you any help you might need—our official resources are considerable. You might care to survey the harbor from one of our helicopters, for instance, or we could fix you up with an office and a typewriter, if you wished. The Port of New York Authority, as you very likely know, is a Bi-State Authority, with the legal status of a public agency, and powers of organization and control which enable it, without cost to the taxpayer, to . . ." (*My mind wandered a little here. What kind of book would it make? A book about a port, a book about a situation, a book about a civilization? Why me, I wondered? Why now? Why New York, anyway?*) ". . . under the ultimate control of the Commissioners, and the executive guidance of the Director of the Port of New York Authority—who is as you know" (Mr. Tobin modestly concluded) "myself."

"I could write what I liked?"

"Of course."

"I could see what I wanted?"

"Naturally. From my own office I can look directly out to the harbor. During the war I used to see your two great *Queen* liners, painted gray, sailing out towards the Narrows and the open sea. They were so fast, you see, that they did not go in convoy, but relied upon their speed to escape the U-boats. It was a fine sight, those great ships sailing out. We never knew whether we would see them back in New York again. I used to be reminded of the guardsman in *Victoria the Great*, no doubt you will remember, who murmured to himself as the Queen passed by on her Jubilee procession, 'Go it, old girl, go it!' I was often much moved myself. Many of us within the Authority have a great pride in our port and what it stands for. It has great romance and historical meaning, you see. It is very beautiful, too."

"Right, Mr. Tobin," said I, concluding my sherry trifle, "that settles it. If it suits you I'll come over and learn more about your port next year, when I've finished a book I'm writing about the climax of the British Empire."

"Excellent," he said. "We shall expect you then, and wish you luck with the Empire. In the meantime I shall see that you are sent some material about the harbor, just to direct your mind, now and then, towards a former colony at latitude 41° North, longitude 74° West, on the far side of the Atlantic."

I remembered the position, as the seasons passed and I wrote my other book, and often I imagined that harbor bustling over there—waiting for me, so I fondly thought now. Pamphlets in air-mail envelopes began to arrive in the spring, together with maps and scholarly books—*The Rise of New York Port, 1850–1861, Metropolitan Transportation, 1980, The Annual Report of the Waterfront Commission, Hub-Bound Travel in the Tri-State Metropolitan Region.* Kind friends sent me picture-postcards of the harbor, or shared their reminiscences of the Staten Island ferry, and an acquaintance at Princeton sent me a review of a reissue of Stokes' *Iconography of Manhattan Island,* a work which, at $795 a set, he thought might come in handy. "The port of New York!" elderly ladies would murmur hazily at tea tables. "Oh, what a fascinating subject for you! Will you have an opportunity, I wonder, to get to know Senator Robert Kennedy, he looks such a *gentleman* I always think, unlike the majority of politicians either here or there. . . ."

In the bath, or on the mountain, I sometimes wondered what relevance the subject had to me and my own people, on the other side of the ocean, that I should carve a chunk from my life to explore it. What was New York harbor to us, or to the world at large? I reasoned out an answer, as the months went by. New York was the Grand Exchange not just of America, but of the world. There all mankind's ideas were inspected, swapped, shuffled, refined or degraded, discarded or made familiar to us all, and there the American dream, which was everybody's dream at heart, simultaneously flowered and shriveled. The greatest passenger ships of the world were all built to connect Europe with this particular port, just as all the thickest red lines on the air-traffic maps led to this same legendary destination. New York is everybody's port. We all think we know that skyline. We have all sailed into Manhattan vicariously, if not with Miss Garbo on the boat deck, then with U Thant on a jet. Everybody's Cousin Jack went to New York in the Navy, everybody's Uncle Pat or Giorgio lives there. Lord Bryce called it "a European city, but of no particular country": now it is a world city, but of no particular race. The movements of New York, the ebb and flow of its historical tides, are the movements of humanity: in the remotest corner of the world the image of a ship entering New York harbor, into the shadow of the skyscrapers, will strike a chord of recognition. New York is foreign to nobody. It is the universal seaport.

And as the summer drew on, I saw that harborfront silhouetted ever more vividly against the huge somber background of a distracted America. Fearful news of hatred and violence reached us from the other shore. I never did get to know Senator Kennedy, for too soon he lay in state in St. Patrick's Cathedral, and letters from friends in Manhattan were full of fear and disillusion. Behind the port, it appeared, the city and the nation were in ferment. I seemed to see Manhattan flickering there upon its wharves, lit up by the fires behind.

"It seems an odd subject for you. What does it mean to

you—as a writer, as an *artist* one might almost say—where's your involvement—where's your, if one might phrase it so, your *emotional interlock?*"

I would take out one of my pamphlets then, and open it at a photograph I often looked at on the sly. The harbor looked cool and gray there, and filled the whole page. A smudge of white smoke half veiled Manhattan. The water was streaked with the wakes of ships, and with rivulets of oil, I suppose, or underwater shoals. In the center a slender bridge stood astride a narrow channel, and all around the edges sprawled the indistinct mass of the city. It looked as though all mankind were edging into view, pressing down to the harbor and the water's edge, to send its energies out beneath the bridge, or welcome reinforcements.

"There's my involvement," I would tell the oaf. "That harbor's mine."

Chapter 2

AROUND
THE GREAT PORT

When I got there, in the fall, an indulgent helicopter pilot
flew me to the geographical center of my subject. Helicopters
are the familiars of New York, its clanking Ariels. They
slide and side-step among the office blocks, they chase their
own shadows across the water, they airily alight, as though
bringing pearls and bonbons to penthouse paramours, upon
the high summits of skyscrapers.

Off the top of a building we fell that day, and sidled
across the Hudson River, and in a few moments the helicopter
stopped, shook itself, and gingerly descended a couple of
hundred feet. Looking out of my side window I found myself
hovering, with a disrespectful clatter, close to the nose of the
Statue of Liberty. That substantial figure of a lady, to quote
one of my favorite guidebook definitions, looked taken
aback: and as our aircraft shifted its angle, so her pallid
head tilted against its background. Now she was set against
a clump of skyscrapers, now against a line of warehouses—
one moment gray institutional buildings on an island, the
next interminable rows of brown houses marching away to
the horizon—a broad river behind her head, as we swung
around her coiffure, and a tangle of suspension bridges,

chimneys, cranes—until, completing our juddery circum-navigation of the statue, I looked at her in full classical profile, and saw her against the sweep of New York Bay.

We hung there for a minute, and the sunshine reflected off the water shone about her head. A ship was sailing steadily out to sea, and a big orange ferryboat pounded back from Staten Island. There lay the freighters at the quarantine station, dejectedly paraded off-shore, and there sped a Coast Guard cutter back to Governors Island. Beyond Jamaica Bay a jet from Kennedy Airport flung itself into the sky. Fragile as ivory stood the Verrazano Bridge above the Narrows, closing the upper bay as a gate into a lagoon, and beyond it lay the silver void of the sea, beyond Sandy Hook and the Ambrose Light, beyond the Ewash Channel and Flynn's Knoll—out past the Gedney Channel, where the Bay turned into the ocean, and the ocean became the world.

I traced the magical names on my map as we hung there, and all my fancies of the last few months began their mutation into fact. Then, with a last curtsy to Liberty, we flew away. "If we hit her we'd be famous," I said to the pilot as we darted off. "What a way to go," he answered. "I'd be the guy that assaulted the Statue of Liberty, and you'd be instant Shakespeare."

Seen from up there, in the bright October sunshine, the reasons for New York looked obvious. Everything below us seemed to be moving—even the skyscrapers, as they shifted one against the next with our momentum. The city looked what it was: a landing place and a bazaar. Every twenty minutes a ship leaves or enters New York. Every day a multitude equivalent to the population of Norway enters its business district. Eight railroad lines end their journeys in the city; expressways circle it, or stalk on stilts across its tenements. One and a half million passengers pass through

Kennedy Airport in an average month—when I was there, 69,000 in a single day.

New York's qualifications are evident, too, when you see it from the air. It might have been man-made as a port, so neatly functional is its shape and situation. On the north-eastern coast of the United States, between latitudes 40° and 41° North, two large chunks of land stand out from the coastline like breakwaters. One is the flank of New Jersey, with its long line of reefs; the other is Long Island in the State of New York, a splendid boulevard, a hundred miles long, of sand, marsh, and grassland. These two land masses approach each other at an angle, and very nearly meet: they are separated by the entrance to New York Bay.

It is a wonderfully sheltered, secretive opening. Long Island protects it from the northern gales, the arm of sand called Sandy Hook reaches out from New Jersey to embrace its channel from the south, and the bulk of Staten Island stands like a cork in the middle. The mariner enters it sailing almost due west, but a few miles from the open sea he turns abruptly north, passes through the bottleneck of the Narrows, leaves Staten Island on his port side, and finds himself in the glorious security of the upper bay—gales and high seas left behind, even the sea birds domesticated, as he steams snugly between Brooklyn and Bayonne towards the comforts of the metropolis.

This is the lordly front door of New York—the carriage sweep. There is a kitchen entrance too, for between Long Island and the mainland there lies Long Island Sound, sixty miles of sheltered water linking the port with the Atlantic by a back route. This will also take a seafarer into the upper bay, via the tidal strait called the East River, while from the American interior the noble Hudson River flows into the Bay out of the north, mingling its icy fresh waters with the salt tide of the Atlantic. Diverse other creeks and rivers debouch into New York Bay, and all around are little islands, inlets, and spits, forming a watery sort of filigree upon the large-scale charts.

In the center of this system of waters stands the island of Manhattan, the core of the port. With its long flat line of shore it provides safe wharfage for many ships: surrounded as it is by water, protected by the Narrows from the open sea, it is a perfect site for a merchant city. It is only just an island, for while the East River and the Hudson bound it east and west, in the north only the insignificant winding stream called the Harlem River separates it from the mainland. But an island it is on the map, an island it looks from a helicopter, it has water at each end of its cross-town streets, and even at its broadest part a determined pedestrian can cross from shore to shore in an hour—ninety minutes, say, if she goes halfway by the cross-town bus.

There is a compact elegance of design to this ensemble. The scale is not very large. Manhattan is ten miles long, and is easily sailed around by stertorous pleasure boats in morning excursions. The islands so importantly named upon the maps are sometimes hardly more than river blobs, and privileged visitors boarding an incoming liner at the Narrows barely have time to polish off a Steak Diane, a Camembert, and a bottle of claret before the ship is swinging into the Manhattan pier, and the longshoremen may be seen hunched over their beer and hot dogs in the sidewalk diner.

It is hard to remember, when the ice floes are crunching down the Hudson, and the ships in harbor are filmed in ice, but by literary standards this is a southern port. A geographically ill-educated poet might look for warm beakers here. New York stands well south of Barcelona, not far north of Lisbon, on more or less the same latitude as Valencia, Athens, or Catania. No warm ocean current enters the Bay, so that it is much colder in winter than any Mediterranean port, and is hardly the sort of haven better-informed visionaries yearn for, when they hear the nightingale; but the harbor is never frozen solid, winter fogs are rare, and sea traffic does not stop for the cold weather, however snarled up the streets of Manhattan. The climate is officially described as *temperate*, but with its miserable extremes of heat, blizzard, and humidity, interspersed with glorious intervals of sparkle, it strikes me rather as *theatrical*.

Dramatic, certainly, almost stagy, are the wide and splendid vistas that extend from the harborfront of New York. Old prints of this bay show it surrounded by rolling hills, but they must have been elevated for artistic effect, because the highest point for miles is Todt Hill on Staten Island, which is 409 feet high. The physical glories of the place are wide, flat glories. The Bay itself is so superbly spacious and serene that early travelers often likened it to the Venetian lagoon. The Atlantic beaches which flank the port seem to run away for ever to disappear in an apotheosis of sea, sun, and sky. The sunsets of New York are the horizontal sort—not just a ball of surly red, plunging down, but slashing sweeps of pink and crimson, mixed up with the last of the evening blue, and the silver off the sea, and the streaks of the wind-swept clouds, to lie like a sumptuous edible from end to end of the horizon.

These are goose landscapes, duck skies. Petrels, egrets, herons, grebe haunt the foreshores of the Bay, and along the migratory flyway that passes over New York travel thousands of birds out of the northern wildernesses—snow geese sometimes in flights of a hundred birds, ducks of many kinds, snow buntings, longspurs from Labrador. Sometimes they are to be seen in haughty formation above the skyscrapers, sweeping south. Before the city was built the Bay and its islands were marvelously rich in wild life. There was venison fat as mutton, wrote a Dutch settler in 1654, pigeons "as thick as sparrows in Holland," oysters so big one cut them into slices. Strawberries and blackberries were the weeds of Manhattan. Bears, wolves, and otters frequented the islands then, seals lay on the foreshore, and the landscapes were green with oaks, walnuts, chestnuts, beeches, and birches. As for the waters of the Bay, they were "well furnished," recorded Daniel Denton in 1670, "with Fish, as Bosse, Sheepsheads, Place, Perch, Trouts, Eels, Turtles and divers others": in 1911, it was reported to the Linnaean Society of New York, 237 species of fish were to be found within fifty miles of the city center.

Even now, to a visitor from more ancient cities, New York seems thinly laid upon its terrain. From the air especially one may see how much dusty green still stipples the place—the treelessness of New York is much exaggerated—and in un-expected corners of the metropolis one may still find the old-fashioned wild flowers that once covered these harbor shores: meadow violet and John's-wort, Queen Anne's lace, bee balm. There is a primeval air to the weird tidal swamps called the Jersey Meadows, which lie within sight of Man-hattan, and are crossed by the New Jersey Turnpike. Brown-ish, soggy, and sullen they lie there, and they make one think of trolls and will-of-the-wisps. A friend of mine was once driving across this gloomy waste with her dog, on her way home to Manhattan on a dark drizzly night. On both sides other cars were racing up the turnpike towards the city. The rain slanted dismally through her headlights, her windshield wipers sadly swished, before, beside, and behind her the traffic relentlessly hastened, when suddenly her dog, with a muffled bark, leapt out of the half-open window. It was as though he could stand it no longer. She caught a last glimpse of his white body, scrambling and slithering through the cars, and then he was lost over the edge of the road, in the darkness of the Meadows. She never saw him again.

"Say, that's a sad story. Never saw him again, huh? Maybe he's still wandering down there. See where the dredge is working? If they could figure out how to drain those Meadows, they'd be worth millions."

Over Jersey City now, a colorless jumble of railway lines and oil tanks, and up the line of the little Hudson River townships, Hoboken and Weehawken and Guttenberg and Union City, straggling down to the water in a welter of boatyards, shabby warehouses, and half-sunken barges. Past them flows the Hudson, one of the great rivers of the world. What an air it has! What consequence! What condescension! A ship is sailing up it now, towards some inland port of the north, and seems to move with a snobbish sniff herself, to be riding such waters. Though it flows to the west of Manhattan, New Yorkers call the Hudson the North River: this is because the old Dutch colonies extended southwards to the Delaware—the Delaware was their South River, the Hudson their North.

There's the George Washington Bridge, monumental between its towers, and now we turn eastward down the runnel of the Harlem River: clutter of Harlem to the right, monotony of Bronx to the left, bridges all the way, the New York Central running in from up-state, a Gothic tower upon a hillock, a great stadium over the railroad tracks. ("Listen, if you're writing about New York you've got to get things straight: Mets is baseball. Jets is football—check?")

Like a fjord into the city Long Island Sound enters from the left, littered with small islands and promontories, comfortably settled all along its shores, and suggesting waterside inns, with clam chowder. Snaking among the suburbs, gradually it turns into the East River, and presently below us there swirls the confluence of currents called Hell Gate, where the Harlem River diffidently adds its stream. Sailing ship captains hated this place. The Dutch first called it Hellegat, and the British were very proud of themselves when they managed to sail a frigate through it during the Revolutionary War.

"We call it the North River when it isn't north, and the East River when it isn't a river. Are we crazy or something?" It doesn't even look like a river, seen from the helicopter. Its water appears to be soupy, as though it needs stirring. Filthy affluents feed it from the bowels of Brooklyn, powerhouse chimneys belch upon its banks, and even the white slab of the United Nations building, flanked by residences of the rich, fails to give it style.

Three suspension bridges, one after the other. They all look much the same from a distance, and few New Yorkers can identify them at sight. "Brooklyn, that's Brooklyn, you can tell by the boardwalk—no, hell, that can't be, that must be Williamsburg. No, wait, I was right, there's the Navy Yard, that's Brooklyn last, *this* is Williamsburg, that's Manhattan in the middle. Okay?" Across the Brooklyn bluffs we clatter, over the long line of the Brooklyn docks, and out towards the open sea—Kennedy Airport to our left, beyond the swampy waters of Jamaica Bay—and so, with the ocean below us, we turn northward again for the grand slam. We have circumhelicopted the port. Ahead of us, gleaming across the Narrows in the morning sun, stands the Verrazano Bridge, the Atlantic gateway to New York, its high arch curving exquisitely beneath blue-gray towers. A white liner is about to pass beneath it, heading for Manhattan. I look at the pilot. He looks at me. "It's not difficult," he says, "there's plenty of room, but you never know when some guy's going to drop a paint-pot off the top. Still, seeing it's a fine day, and you're writing a book . . ."

So, like a very determined insect, nose up in the sunshine, we swoop beneath the span of the bridge. High above us rises its great steel arch, and as we pass through its shadow, so does the liner. For a moment we travel side by side in exuberant partnership, the passengers waving excitedly from the sundeck and even the officer on the flying bridge allowing himself a salute: and we see before us, across the waters of the upper bay, the skyscrapers of the inner city.

There stands Manhattan like an island keep, a fortress of power, talent, greed, and beauty. Elderly ships' captains tell me they never lose the excitement of this moment, as they turn the corner of the Narrows beneath the bridge, and see this sight before them. Tired commuters taking the ferry home to Staten Island still stand silent on the windy stern to watch the lights of Manhattan retreat into the night. Blasé diplomatists flying in from Europe press their noses to the window, when the towers of New York are sighted through the haze. We read of voyagers dropping dead of heart attacks, like pilgrims reaching Mecca, or explorers crossing the thresholds of Lhasa. In one of his films Charlie Chaplin has a shipload of immigrants forcibly restrained by police officers from showing too much enthusiasm, as they sail past the Statue of Liberty into this port.

The pilot has nothing to say, but soon the high towers rise before and around us, a million windows gleaming, and there are tugs and scows and motorboats scurrying about the piers, and millions of cars and buses and people in the shadowy cavities between the buildings, and jams of trailer-trucks in back streets, and the skyscrapers toppling above our rotors, and a dazzle of steel and aluminum, and a glare of reflected sunshine, and here and there below us those little clouds of white steam, issuing from the central heating systems of the metropolis, which help to give this seaport its suggestion of volcanic force and omen.

Chapter 3

THE SUCCESSION

I had noticed, dotted around the perimeters of Manhattan, the power stations of the Consolidated Edison Company— "Con Ed" in the vernacular, or the demonology—disagreeably smoking down the years. Observing these plants from a distance sometimes suggested to me, if I tried very hard, encampments upon the Manhattan shore, shad or sturgeon baking over the campfire, wigwams above the beach. For I was struck from the start by the transience of New York, its sense of passing parade, and wandered for a time around the city seeing everywhere the succession of its rulers and inhabitants. New York has not done much to preserve its past, and has traditionally been fonder of change than of preservation. "It'll be a fine city when it's finished," as an old joke says. Nowadays, though, the place is full of preservation groups, archaeological societies, and nostalgic aficionados of the past, and I found before long that any inquiry into the origins of the port aroused a sentimental enthusiasm; so that gradually, prodding my imagination always with old prints and antiquarian advice, and often joining the park philosophers for periods of meditation, I overlaid the New

York scene, so to speak, with multiple exposures, and so observed for myself the printing of the port.

I saw for a start, in the tipsy course of Broadway down Manhattan Island, the tracks of the aboriginal Indians who first lived around this bay. This long street, loitering through the stern grid of the modern city, brings to the metropolitan layout a welcome taste of frailty. Buses traveling down it do queer zigzag things at intersections, and it wobbles right and left across the numerical pattern, now bumping into Tenth Avenue in the west, now rebounding across the island to collide with Fourth in the east. Fifth Avenue is a far grander boulevard, one of the loftiest streets indeed on earth, but it is one of your bureaucratic streets—like Moskovsky Prospekt in Leningrad, which actually runs along a meridian. Broadway springs out of nature and of history.

Down this trail the Indians used to travel to the Bay, sometimes swerving to avoid a thicket or a pool, sometimes fording a marsh, keeping to the familiar water's edge until, around 71st Street, they swung to the east to take a short cut through the forest to the southern tip. I am assured that even in those dim aboriginal days Manhattan's function was established. It was already an island of portage and exchange. People traveling from Long Island to New Jersey would stop on the island to indulge in a little commerce or ceremonial; people from the north would go down to fish or exchange their goods; and it was more or less on the site of Wall Street, one incorrigible romantic assured me, that the clam shells which were the standard medium of exchange found their proper economic level.

Certainly it was a cosmopolitan island from the beginning. The Indians of New York apparently belonged to several distinct subtribes of the Algonquins. Some were Wappinger

Indians, some were Delaware Indians, and they all spoke different dialects. They generally only came to Manhattan in the warm weather: but then, in the humid hush of the New York summer, the woods rustled with the activities of these misty primitives, greeting each other with sign language or tribal shrieks, I suppose, exchanging game for fish, deerskins for sea shells, and occasionally loping up the Broadway war-path to cross cudgels with the brooding savages of Westchester.

I cannot pretend to have seen these people very vividly, as I looked for their shades and traces in the city. I thought of them often, as I tramped along Broadway myself, and sometimes I saw an unmistakable Indian face in the streets of the port, smooth and introspective still: but they did not leave much behind—only an occasional legend, the meander of a single street, and a few place names: Hoboken, Weehawken, possibly Manhattan itself.

I caught no glimpse of Leif, son of Eric the Red, whose longship is claimed to have been the first ocean vessel to make landfall in New York. But often, on crystal spring mornings, I made out the French caravel *Dauphine*, 100 tons, lying at the head of the lower bay, just beyond the Narrows —no bigger than a tug, only a blur against the green woodlands of Staten Island. She was the first European vessel whose arrival in New York is historically certain, and she must have been a staggering sight to the watching Indians on the foreshore—an inexplicable product of advanced technology, from some altogether unsuspected world.

It was 1524. The commander of the *Dauphine* was an Italian, Giovanni da Verrazano, who was looking for the Northwest Passage to China on behalf of the French king. He had worked his way up the Atlantic coast, perhaps from

Florida, and he was struck by the tranquillity of this silent anchorage. He took a boat through the Narrows into the upper bay, and was courteously received by the Indians, who came out to meet him in their canoes, apparently wishing to act as guides, or perhaps having propositions to make about exchange rates. He saw the mouth of the Hudson—"an exceeding great stream of water"—guessed there were minerals in the hills around the Bay, took soundings, and thought the general prospect "commodious and delightful." "Any laden ship," he reported to his patron, could enter the harbor. A storm blew up though, Verrazano returned to the *Dauphine*, and nobody went ashore. In the morning they were gone.

As explorers often do, Verrazano gave proprietory names to everything, brief though his visit was, and perfunctory his survey. He claimed it all on behalf of France. He named the upper bay the Gulf of Santa Margherita, after the King of France's sister. He named the Hudson the River Vendôme, after an influential French duke. He called the whole area Angoulême, after the King of France's princely honorific. But all these professional gestures were unavailing. The names never stuck, the French never ruled New York, and Verrazano was presently eaten by Caribs in Brazil.

Much more substantial is the figure of Henry Hudson, the Englishman who arrived eighty-five years later in the service of the Dutch. We can all see *him*. His little ship, the *Half Moon*, does not lie diffident outside the Narrows, but anchors comfortably off the point of Manhattan, attended by the canoes of the Indians like a cruise ship among bumboats— "eight and twentie Canoes full of men, women and children . . . some in Mantles and Feathers, and some in Skinnes of divers sorts of good furres." A homely crew of Dutchmen and Britons peers down from the deck, occasionally bickering with one another, and sometimes bartering beads and knives for the Indians' tobacco leaves. The ship's boats busily take soundings in the Bay, and all is diligent activity and seamanship.

Hudson thought the river itself—that "exceeding great stream of water"—might be the passage to China, and he sailed cautiously up it as far as the site of Albany—"the end of the River's Navigablenesse." Altogether he spent a month inside Sandy Hook; but he went home to Europe a disappointed man, having failed to find the China route, and three years later he too disappeared for ever when his mutinous crew set him adrift in an open boat in the icy waters of the north. But he has stood high in the New York Pantheon ever since, the earliest lion of the city's Anglo-Saxon Establishment. Like a proper American, he did not fiddle about with royal courtesies, and worked impartially for British and Dutch employers; like a true New Yorker, he spotted the value of the fur trade in these parts, took the trouble to sail upstream, and so first envisaged New York Bay as a place of commerce. When, three hundred years later, they decided to honor the anniversary of his visit, the New Yorkers did it in style. A fleet of warships from all over the world dropped anchor in his river, extending from 47th Street to 222nd Street in the city of New York, and a replica of the *Half Moon* was towed ceremonially upstream by a tug. Paddle steamers, ferryboats, liners, yachts, schooners, and steam tugs circled around the anchored fleet, and Hudson's memory was honored with a sybaritic series of banquets and the very first flight of an airplane over New York—navigated by Wilbur Wright in person.

The Dutch, fired by Hudson's reports, were the first European settlers in New York, and their presence lingers. From 1610 to 1665 Dutchmen ran this port, as an outpost of New Netherlands. They bought the island of Manhattan from the Indians with cloth, hatchets, and odds and ends to the value of sixty guilders—forty dollars, say: though who were the swindlers it is hard to say, for the Indians had no title to the island anyway. They sailed through the East River into Long Island Sound. They opened up the fur trade, and sent their bargainers far up the Hudson. They built a little town on lower Manhattan, with a fort, a courthouse, a prison, a coroner's court, and most other essentials of life in America. They built the first of the New York ships, launching her in 1614, and prophetically naming her *Onrust* —*Restless*.

The Dutch, it seemed to me as I pursued their memories around the harbor, gave to New York its taste for solid profit. They may not have been dashing, but they knew the value of money, and no petty inhibitions of race or ideology impeded their pursuit of it. Their New York was a melting pot from the start. Most of the first settlers were not Dutch at all, but Walloon refugees from the Spanish Netherlands, and by 1643 they were said to include "four or five hundred men of eighteen different languages." By the 1690s even the Jews were prospering on Manhattan, and had their own synagogues and cemetery—a little to the north, it is reliably surmised, of Wall Street. The infrastructure of commerce was established then: wharves, banks, brokers' offices. New Amsterdam was perhaps a lofty title for the little settlement, which never sent more than 85,000 skins a year home to Holland; but the Dutch created New York as an emporium, and thus set its tone for ever.

Several other lasting characteristics were initiated then. Subtleties of real estate, trade monopolies, a bent for tax evasion, a taste for strong liquor—all these New York traits are recognizable in New Amsterdam. It was a company town, governed by the Dutch West India Company, and it had a cosmopolitan, capitalist effervescence denied the pious English colonies of Virginia and New England. It also had a weakness for violence. As for its most famous Governor, the one-legged Peter Stuyvesant, he was the original city Boss, with his lavish official mansion on the East River, his private property uptown, the seven city streets named for members of his family, his crooked secretary, his ferocious prejudices, and his folksy nickname—Peg-Leg Pete. I took a dislike to the fellow.

For generations the merchant aristocracy of New York was largely Dutch, and even now a few grand old dames, I am told, glorying in the multi-syllabic names of the burghers, look down upon the upstart Jews and English. I used to imagine them sitting alone in vast overheated dining rooms, eating raw herring and boiled potatoes beneath brown ancestral portraits, and I loved to come across their fruity patronymics—Schermerhorns, Van Cortlandts, Beekmans, Bayards. Brooklyn Heights used to be a favorite neighborhood of the old Dutch families, and it pleased me to fancy them up there still, lapped in all the comforts of filial respect and merchant prosperity, when I saw those big brownstone houses, high above the East River, through the deep gulf of Wall Street.

The Dutch made and named that street, the site of a protective rampart across the island, and on the map of New York they have left their stamp everywhere: in Nieuwe Haarlem, in Zand Hoek, in the Bowerij, in Hellegat, in the borough named after Jonas Bronck or the district that once owed allegiance to a young Dutch milord—*jonkheer* in the vernacular. Their English rivals often treated them with contempt, talking of Dutch courage and Dutch comfort—meaning thank God it's no worse. White Hall was the nickname they mockingly gave Stuyvesant's palace: and Whitehall Street it remains, perversely, to this day—from Battery Point to Bowling Green.

God-fearing though the English settlements were, on each flank of New Netherlands, still the British were a perfect pest to the Dutch. In Europe England and Holland were cutthroat competitors; in America the English colonies gradually outstripped the Dutch in wealth and numbers, so that towards the end of their rule the colonists of New Amsterdam must have felt themselves besieged by sanctimonious louts. Year by year the English crept towards the settlement, northward through New Jersey, westward through Long Island. English officials made a fuss about boundary rights. English traders filched business. English pirates infested the seas. English Quakers infiltrated New Amsterdam to spread pernicious doctrines, very unpopular with Governor Stuyvesant. English statesmen periodically insisted that the Dutch had no right to be there at all. In 1653 Oliver Cromwell actually fitted out an expedition to seize the place, during one of the Anglo-Dutch wars in Europe, but peace was signed just in time; after the Restoration Charles II, coolly proclaiming the whole of New Netherlands to be English territory, announced that in future the colony of New Amsterdam would form part of the estate of his brother, the Duke of York.

In August 1664 a squadron of four British warships anchored just outside the Narrows, off Coney Island, and an officer was rowed to Manhattan under a white flag of truce. Taken to Stuyvesant in his palace, he demanded the town's instant surrender. Stuyvesant furiously refused; the English returned to their ships; next day the squadron passed the Narrows, sailed unopposed through the upper bay, and bore down upon Manhattan. The position of the Dutch was forlorn. Their defenses were feeble, their morale was low, and most of them wanted to surrender. Only old Stuyvesant, it appears, still blustered his defiance. Legend has him standing upon a wall of the fort at Battery Point, as the English ships sailed in, and it is easy to envisage him there. A fort stands on the site still—Fort Clinton—and from its walls one can still survey the whole broad sweep of the upper bay, and face up to the approaching ships. There stands Stuyvesant, stamping his wooden leg, and ignoring the appeals of chaplains and anxious burghers. He is ordered to hold New Amsterdam, he says, and hold it he will, even against its own wishes. As the warships come within range, he gives the order to open fire. The first gunner stands with lighted taper; the order to shoot is awaited; at that very moment there arrives a petition from ninety-three leading citizens of the city, including one of the Governor's own sons, begging him to surrender. Peg-Leg Pete gives in at last. He orders the gunner to quench his flame, and the white flag is run up. "I had rather be carried to my grave," murmurs Stuyvesant theatrically, but in fact the old fraud retires to his country place on the Bowery, and lives happily ever after under the English.

So New York was born. To the English it was essentially a harbor from the beginning, secondary to Boston and Philadelphia, but full of promise. "The growingest town in America," was how Lord Bellemont described it in 1698, and Governor Robert Hunter, writing home to Dean Swift in 1710, said it was "the finest air to live upon in the universe." The English treated the Dutch fairly on the whole, allowing them to keep their religion, their customs, and their property, and the city too preserved its original character— volatile, cosmopolitan, greedy. It was three-quarters Dutch in 1664, with the rest a mixture of English, French, Scandinavian, Portuguese, and Negro slaves. Dutch and English were both generally spoken. For fifteen months in the 1670s, during another Anglo-Dutch war, New York actually became Dutch again, and was renamed New Orange; but the English returned after the war, and gradually they imposed their own style upon the place, elevating it year by year to be a proper all-round seaport.

In those days it was unmistakably a city of the sea, and must have been very like one of the contemporary Atlantic ports of England—Bristol, or Liverpool. It was rich in maritime taverns, *The Anchor and Bollards, The Three Jolly Sailors, At the Sign of the Fry'd Oyster;* one of the most famous was on the spit at Sandy Hook, where captains would often run ashore for an ale and a chop in passage. The growing wealth of the city was linked inescapably with the sea. Merchants replaced landowners as the aristocracy of New York: the churchwardens of Trinity Church, the cathedral of the English Establishment, were empowered to "seize up and secure all wrecks and drift whales and whatever else drives from the high sea and is then left below high tide having no rightful owner." In 1678 18 vessels of one sort or another were registered at the port of New York; by 1694 there were 162. New York played a useful part in the British scheme of a self-sufficient Empire, shipping its own goods in its own ships from one colony to another, swapping foods for raw materials, slaves for manufactured goods. As the farmlands of the interior were developed New York became a port of agricultural export. It sent flour to the rich sugar islands of the British West Indies, and with the proceeds bought the goods it needed in England. Thus it contributed both to the sustenance of the British Empire and to its prosperity.

English New York thrived also with piracy, providing markets and diversions for English buccaneers, when they wallowed in deep with booty from the French. Kidd was a well-known man-about-town, until they took him home and hanged him, and Benjamin Fletcher, Governor in the 1690s, was close friends with another enterprising cutthroat, Captain

Thomas Tew of the *Amity* ("I wished in my mind," wrote His Excellency, explaining this disturbing intimacy, "to make him a sober man, and in particular to reclaim him from the vile habit of swearing. I gave him a book to that purpose"). Very early, too, New York became a mail port—the western terminus of the British Government's packet service from Falmouth in Cornwall. By 1776 it ranked fourth among American ports, surpassed only by Philadelphia, Boston, and Charleston; for the English knew all about harbors, and they recognized New York to be one of the great havens of the world.

To a Briton the downtown area of Manhattan still seems familiar ground. In the streets of the shipowners, the great merchants, and the harbor men, I feel more or less at home. Immense buildings loom over the scene, of course, and cast a shadow upon the island that could only be American; but in and among them run the twisty streets of the English, with names like Gold Street and Maiden Lane, and fine old smells of coffee and draught beer. Handsome Georgian churches stand in moldering churchyards, presided over still by clergymen of impeccable Episcopalian orthodoxy. Financiers emerging from stock exchanges occasionally wear bowler hats. Pedestrian discipline is reassuringly shaky. One often hears English accents, and faces look more nearly English than elsewhere, especially when seen through the steamy Dickensian windows of chophouses or oyster bars. Everywhere there are reminders of the old sea trade with England, for so many generations the staple of New York— house flags above classical porticoes, models of beloved old liners, stiff-collared Commodores of the Line in framed assembly down the corridors of shipping offices. "Good morning," I said in my best London manner, to a man in a striped tie and a terribly British suit, whom I swore I recognized in an elevator one day. "Hi there," he replied, shooting his cuffs to show his onyx cuff links.

Long after the Revolution, old pictures show, New York still looked like an English seaport, and there are occasional vistas that suggest it still—the solitary spires that rise above the rooftops of Brooklyn, for instance, or the rambling red brick houses of Saint George on Staten Island, seen from a hazy distance. In the early years of the Republic this was still a low-built city of gentle prospects. Its architectural tone was set by the mercantile jungle at the bottom end of Manhattan, with pleasant rows of Georgian houses and green country hills in sight. There is a picture of Broadway and Bowling Green, drawn in 1826, which looks as elegant and leisurely as Bath itself, in the languid muslined poses of its ladies, the sweet innocence of the children beneath their parasols, and the dogs besporting themselves upon the cobblestones.

I looked hard for relics of this pre-industrial American idyl, and found lots. Gracie Mansion is one, the official residence of the Mayor of New York which stands among gardens on the banks of the East River: it is a well-proportioned house of white clapboard, sensitively extended in recent years, with shutters, balconies, and wide steps down to its lawn—once the manor house of those parts, and still looking less like a perquisite of political office than the retreat of some cultivated merchant, prospering upon gentlemanly commodities like spice or slaves. Here and there in Manhattan stand terraces of Georgian town houses, their style all too often ruined by the protuberances of air conditioners and the undefinable emanation of too much money. Pleasant little classical churches, too, survive among the skyscrapers, and there are many happy examples of what James Fenimore Cooper once described as "a species of second-rate genteel houses that abound in New York, into which I have looked when passing with the utmost pleasure"—which I recognized with pleasure, too, when I came across their modest façades, their dormers, and their fanlights, squeezed between overbearing office blocks, overlaid with Victoriana, cut in half and commercially disguised, or lovingly cherished by intellectuals. Most evocative of all, I found one day on a bluff above the Brooklyn Navy Yard a solitary white house inhabited by admirals. It has green shutters and green lawns and green creepers up its walls, and coming across it unwarned among the docks and brown desolations of Brooklyn, I almost expected to hear minuets issuing from it, or the softer thud of croquet balls among the steam hammers.

I loved the echoes of that young American seaport, from the days when the settlements around the Bay must have sparkled with the high spirits of independence; but presently that formidable new man, the American, dismissed the delicacy from his harbor, and got down to brass tacks. Away went the finicky English ornaments. Down came the pleasant terraces, one by one. The grid system of streets was laid upon Manhattan, like so many delivery lines down to the waterfront. In the mercantilist system of the British Empire New York had been a place of middling importance. Calcutta, Bombay, or the Caribbean ports all meant more to the imperial structure. It was the Revolution that made New York a great force in the world. For thirty years the seaport faltered, hampered by hostilities with Britain, by wars elsewhere in the world, and by uncertain rivalries within the infant Union. But in 1815 the news of the Treaty of Ghent, reaching New York seven weeks after its signing, ushered the harbor into its own. Trade and commerce freed at last, all the seaways open, the New Yorkers seized their opportunities with furious enterprise, and made this place the first seaport of the Americas.

The Victorian era created the New York we know. The flood of goods, immigrants, and cash that poured into the New World from Europe was channeled chiefly through this ever-open port. The cutting of the Erie Canal, connecting the Hudson River with the Great Lakes, made it the chief outlet of the prairie country and the explosive Middle West. The cotton trade of the South was ingeniously diverted to New York, the cotton being transshipped at Manhattan for delivery to Europe. Other foreign trade was won from Boston and Philadelphia by gusto, skill, and guile. The ebullience of the early nineteenth-century New York shipowners was proverbial. They were called the Peep o' Day Boys, so early in the morning did they appear at the Battery, to watch for their arriving argosies, and if a reluctant captain pleaded lack of wind as an excuse for delaying departure, the standard reply was curt: "Go and *find* wind!"

New York was the prime patron of the clipper ships, so often to be seen scudding flamboyantly through the Narrows from China or San Francisco; the word "skyscraper," associated in everyone's mind with the towers of Manhattan, was the old name for a topsail. For a time the steamship lines of New York were masters of the transatlantic traffic, and into New York Bay, between 1836 and 1910, sailed some twenty million immigrants in the greatest human migration in history. South Street, the waterfront of lower east Manhattan, became a power in the world, for there the shipping industry had its headquarters, and the meaning of the port was concentrated: one spoke generically of South Street then, as of Wall Street or Rialto.

Now the railways spread westward from New York, ancillaries to the harbor, and the first of the great suspension bridges bound together the edges of the Bay, and the skyscrapers rose upon the foreshore. As the world wars weakened the old European ports, so New York rose to supreme power and wealth. As the whole land mass of America sprang to life, so this seaport became the supply base of a new world, where the money could be raised, the engineers hired, the steel shipped. Wall Street became the financial capital of the

Western world. Buoyantly surviving conflicts and catastrophes, absorbing into its presence millions of bewildered foreigners, combining immense wealth with desperate poverty, dedicated always to change and movement and speed, New York became a port like no other, behind whose wharves and warehouses there evolved a civilization of sumptuous luxury and finesse, cross-grained with violence.

Here my final picture, absorbing into its composition all those faded vignettes of the past, emerged in all too vivid color; and having it clear now in my mind how salt-streaked and maritime were the origins of New York, I set out to explore the lie of the sea.

Chapter 4

THE LIE
OF THE SEA

As I say, like most visitors to New York I had not generally taken much notice of the sea, regarding it only as a spectacular backdrop for the skyscrapers, or a setting for the Statue of Liberty. Now my view of the city began to change: Manhattan was no longer an isolated prodigy for me, but a single component of the great Bay complex, and I realized more sharply how imminent was the salt water at the end of every cross-town street. One day I strolled from the spine of the island to its western foreshore; and holding my notebook in my hand, I recorded the signs and graffiti of my progress, from Fifth Avenue to the Hudson piers.

They were very posh signs at first, of course, in the opulent heart of the island, among the scented stores and the unattainable apartments—*Exclusive to Us,* for instance, *Lady Members' Entrance, Tailors to the Gentry Since 1836, The Vicar Will Hear Confessions Himself on the Third Sunday in Every Month.* Then I passed into the theater district, and found myself in a blaze of superlatives and innuendoes— Mightiest, Tenderest, Riskiest—*Biggest Steaks in Town, Freshest Maine Lobster,* FIFTEEN KILLED IN EXPLOSION, *Best Books in Back*—"I Laughed Till I Cried," "The Most Moving,

Direct and Disturbing Theatrical Experience of the Season," "A Sizzling Exposure," "Vintage Ibsen," *Adults Only*.

Down, or up, in the world I went, into that layer of New York which seems to be in a constant fretful process of demolition, where the brownstone terraces are interrupted by blank side walls and parking lots, where the faded cards tucked behind the bell pushes announce a rear-guard action of respectability, and where the construction lots are guarded, so a notice told me, by *Attack Dogs—Trained by Canine Etiquette Inc*. Here a first suggestion of flotsam struck me, in the foreign names and the raffish air. Here Save Our Homes Inc. announced itself Affiliated to the Puerto Rican Community Development Project, and Duk Sung Son invited registration at his Karate School. Troy the Village Boy Loved Doris. Crabtree, Composer-Philosopher, in the Midst of *Domestic Turmoil*, announced an *Artistic Festival* to Add a Tranquil Note to Human Lives. *In the Eternal Flame Is All Wisdom*, said a graffito on a wall; *Live Models for Photography*, retorted a lugubrious billboard man. I jotted down the luncheon choice in a restaurant—nothing uncommon to a New Yorker, but heady stuff for me. Veal Parmigian with Spaghetti, it ran, London Broil and 2 Veg., Mozzarella Cheeseburger with French Fries, Southern Fried Chicken, Cheese Blintzes.

And finally, pencil always at the ready, I passed beneath the stark elevated highway that runs beside the Hudson in those parts, and found myself in the messy, drab, and crowded streets behind the docks, where the trucks were noisily maneuvering themselves out of inaccessible alleys, drivers hanging precariously from their cabs to watch the trailers swing around, and the longshoremen were hunched, matchsticks in the corners of their mouths, on the chrome and plastic stools of smoky brown bars. Here were the signs of the sea. The Manhattan piers are not much to look at, just at the moment, but they are magically inscribed. On the pierhead buildings were the proud old names of transatlantic travel—Cunard, Holland-America, North German Lloyd, The Columbus Line ("Continuing the Traditions of the Proudest Name in Seamanship"). On the notice boards I found the rosters of the longshoremen, the Rafferties and Roches and Albertinis of the waterfront pedigree, and on the arrival boards were chalked the names of the ocean liners— those spirited ocean names which are the last permissible flourish of jingo, names of nations, names of great men, names of queens or myths or distant places. *Steamships Supplied*, it said in old-fashioned lettering on a delivery truck. *No Scabs*, growled a warning on a wall.

Now I saw the water itself, brownish and scummy among the piers, and the shapes of the ships themselves were above me, and stenciled crates spoke of bananas from Guatemala or turbine parts from Germany. I ended my walk in a ship chandler's, a shop remote indeed from the delights of Saks or Bonwit Teller, but hardly less seductive. No crested appointment to royalty, I thought, could be grander than this establishment's credentials: "Purveyors of Ships' Stores since the Days of the Sailing Ships." Tiffany or Abercrombie and Fitch never sold objects more alluring than the binnacles, chronometers, toggles, tarpaulins, and radar screens on display there, and I doubt if Parke-Bernet ever auctioned finer titles than these: *Hints for Master Mariners, The Bluejacket's Manual, Questions and Answers for Third Mates*. I always enjoy the suavity of a really sophisticated shop assistant's approach, inquiring if you would care to have the Tang horses taken out of their cabinet, or try the mink on, but I know no grander opening gambit than the one I overheard in the chandler's that day:

"When you sailin', captain?"

But it is off the normal shopping routes, and not many of New York's visitors, or even residents, often walk down to the working waterfront. A distant glimpse of navigation lights, the remote passing of a liner from the office window, perhaps a Sunday excursion around Manhattan or across the Bay to Staten Island—such is the sum of the average New Yorker's acquaintance with his port.

The early Americans, especially the New Englanders, were among the finest sailors in the world, and the original United States was consciously a maritime Power. Its Founding Fathers were all from seaboard regions, and the very first legislation of the first Congress, meeting in 1789 not half a mile from the New York waterfront, was intended to encourage American shipping. Few Americans were born far from the sea: most of them sprang from seagoing stock, Dutch, English, or Scandinavian. In those days the world considered New York first of all a seaport, and so did its citizens. The very name of the city was synonymous with racy seamanship: many a time did an English captain, daring the utmost head of sail upon his vessel, find himself overhauled by some irrepressible New York skipper flaunting a downright improper spread of canvas.

Perhaps it was the opening of the West that turned the Americans away from the ocean—or the end of slavery— or the influx of landlubber immigrants—or the new sense of national self-sufficiency—or the taste for isolation. Whatever it was, there seems to have been a distinct revulsion of feeling in the second half of the nineteenth century. New York shipowners, so triumphant in the age of sail, were unexpectedly left behind in the age of steam, and seldom competed very resolutely in the heyday of the transatlantic passenger competition. Sailoring is a demanding life at best, and the slow spread of affluence among Americans made it harder to find first-class men willing to work in the backbreaking squalor of the old steamships—whose splendors, as they sailed so majestically out to sea, were often supported by gangs of nearly naked stokers working like slaves to the beat of a rhythmic gong, in the loathsome furnace-quarters far below. By the end of the century only one in every ten American merchant seamen was a United States citizen, and the New York piers were dominated by foreign shipping. In 1865 455 foreign steamships entered New York, in 1882 1,945; by 1910 less than 10 per cent of the port's foreign commerce was carried in U. S. bottoms.

Even now the world does not really think of the United States as a maritime nation, as we think of Britain, Holland, or Norway. Her great navies may patrol the oceans from Villefranche to the China coast, and up the Hudson River there lies, forlornly mothballed in midstream, a reserve fleet of merchant vessels itself larger than most fleets of the world —rank upon rank of aging freighters, huddled together for comfort as obsolescence creeps up. Potentially the United States can summon to her service more ships than any other country, not to speak of men and money; yet the American maritime heritage is curiously neglected, and there is not much public pride in it. Angry admirals often rumble about this negligence, and sometimes politicians make an issue of it: even Mayor La Guardia, a landsman if ever there was one, felt it necessary in 1941 to remind his fellow citizens of "the dominant part the sea has always played in the affairs of New Yorkers."

I was puzzled by this lack of interest in New York. It seemed to me you could spend a month in Manhattan, your conversation ranging over the whole field of affairs, drugs to slums to Vietnam, without hearing the sea mentioned, or arguing a single maritime issue. The mystic empathy that so often links Europeans to the sea seems altogether lacking here: I only heard of one ritual affirmation—a ceremony at

Epiphany, when the Greek Orthodox Archbishop of New York throws a wooden cross into the Hudson, and members of his church dive after it. In many ways New York is the least maritime city I know. It is certainly the least maritime of ports. Most New Yorkers look as though they have never set eyes on a ship, and I remember vividly the quandary of a very average Brooklyn family, when I saw them set foot on a tug for the first time. Whether to be casual or innocent was the issue, whether to swagger up the gangplank with a nautical roll, or whether to approach the experience in a spirit of comical naïveté—"Say, is that what they call a porthole?" Some, pursuing one tactic, were dressed in vaguely nautical gear, bell-bottoms and peaked caps, while the rest were wearing the highest of possible heels, and moved to a tinkle of small ornaments. I could not help being flattered when this motley company, finding me in the pilothouse wearing my hair rather too long, talking in an ineffably English accent, eating an apple and carrying the *Village Voice* under my arm, asked me if I was the captain.

The adjectives that normally go with seaports—robust, breezy, hearty—scarcely apply to New York. This is not only temperament, but topography too, for the New Yorkers have largely wrecked their own waterfronts, and shut the sea breezes out. There was seldom a more wonderfully situated metropolis, set upon its double bay within sight of the ocean, with the ships docking just down the road from the concert halls and couturiers. It is still a thrilling fact that the largest of the world's liners tie up within a mile of the Metropolitan Opera House—"as though one of our ships were to sail," a Cunard man once suggested to me, "bang up Piccadilly to dock in Trafalgar Square." There are lesser capitals—Stockholm, Reykjavik—where the ships come even closer to the center of things, and the parliamentarian emerging from his debate may see the prow of a freighter almost immediately outside the legislative door, to prod him into support for shipping subsidies; but I know of no other supreme metropolis where the ships lie so intimately close to the heart of urban life.

Yet there are astonishingly few places in New York where a citizen can get down to the dockside proper without at least discomfort and at worst trespass. For one thing those gloomy streets behind the wharves, often still cobbled and always perilous with trucks, scarcely encourage the serendipitist. For another the Manhattan expressways, now high on piles above the city, now at water level, insulate the city from its shoreline, and clamp its people inside. Higher up the Hudson, well above the docks, there are riverside parks and recreation areas, but even they have an improving air to them, a civic air, are discreetly laid out with bicycle tracks and marble columns, and breathe nothing of the swagger, the vulgarity, the sweat, the seafood, the history, and the beer that ought to go with seaport waterfronts. They are bravely trying to preserve part of the South Street waterfront as a seaport museum; but there conformity of another kind is creeping in, creators of folk jewelry and driftwood are moving into the old sail lofts, and a café announces itself as "New York's hip underground culture den on the groovy Right Bank."

It is almost as though New York is ashamed of its origins. "What's it to me?" as a man on the subway said to me one evening. "A lot of nuts killing each other on the waterfront, and a few rich guys with ships. So who'ya trying to interest? So where's your audience? (Excuse me, I get off here, Thirty-fourth Street. No offense meant. . . .)"

None taken, either, though I longed to convince him how wrong he was, for the farther I wandered in my task the saltier I found the place to be. Everywhere creeks and inlets edged into the city, to remind me that I was on the shores of one of those damp labyrinths, mazed about with marshes and rivulets, where a great river enters the sea. The more I looked, the less unlikely seemed the tales of marine life I found in the natural-history books: the great sea turtles who sometimes saunter through the Narrows, the sturgeon big as men who still ascend the Hudson River, or the brook trout found swimming in a gutter on 58th Street, when a water main burst in 1956. This really is, despite first impressions, an amphibious city.

It is cut about with water, as though the Hudson, the Sound, and the Bay are perpetually hoping to unite: in the eighteenth century the East River and the Hudson actually did meet at high tide, somewhere in the vicinity of Canal Street, until they put a sewer through. Verrazano reported innumerable Indians in little boats "going from one part to another," and a resolute tourist with a little boat could still visit some unexpected districts of the city. Where the East River meets the Sound, in particular, the land is threaded about with channels and straits, so that the stranger seldom knows which bridge goes where, whether it is open sea before him, or only another unscheduled creek.

What is more, they are constantly shifting the lie of the sea. Here the garbage of Manhattan is shoveled repulsively into the water as land fill. There dredgers are scooping a new channel. Many of New York's waterways are man-made, or at least humanly improved. Hell Gate was far more perilous to navigate until, in the 1860s, they blew up some of its rocks. The Harlem River was not navigable at all, even by small craft, until in 1895 they cut a channel through the shoal called Spuyten Duyvil, at the Hudson end (the old river course was filled in, and administratively a small slice of Manhattan remains within its loop, separated by a vanished geographical fact from its hinterland in the Bronx).

I poked in a baffled way among many of these waterways: obscure inlets like Saw Mill Creek or Dead Horse Bay, that speak of the pioneers; shining flats and shallows of Jamaica Bay, rippled by the passing jets; the twisting lesser rivers, seeping through the suburbs and factories, which flow into the Bay out of the mainland—the Hackensack, the Passaic, the Raritan, the Rahway; the streams that drain the marshes of the Jersey Meadows, stained with chemical refuse, oil scum, and decayed animal matter; the secretive inlets which still give a rural sea charm to the shores of Staten Island; the big tidal straits, Arthur Kill and Kill van Kull, up which the tankers pass, and in whose shallows lie the abandoned hulks of this port, the dead tugs and the superannuated scows, the ribbed hulls of old barges, the skeletons of schooners.

Of them all, the most peculiar are the hangdog creeks by which the sea finds its way into the very heart of urban Brooklyn. One of these is the Gowanus Canal, a short and gloomy tongue of water, lined with blackened derelict wharves, which runs up from the harbor behind the Brooklyn piers, slouches beneath a bridge or two, and very soon gives up. The other is the Newtown Creek, which strikes me as the most awful stretch of water I have ever seen. It forms the boundary between the boroughs of Queens and Brooklyn, and was once claimed to be the busiest waterway in the world, carrying more traffic in three miles than the Mississippi in three thousand.

I made my way to this Stygian brook by car, meandering through the blighted Brooklyn back streets, where the sliced rumps of houses are shored up in expectation of approaching expressways, and the long lines of tenements seem to heave up and down those slight eminences in the tarmac that are the sole evidence of the Brooklyn hills beneath. Through dumps and waste yards we went, haunted by the smells of tannery and crude oil, around the ruins of deserted terraces, down evil streets where the Negro children merrily played, until we saw the Brooklyn-Queens Expressway, off to our right, suddenly rearing into the black cage of a cantilever bridge. This the driver recognized, not without relief. "Somewhere down there that creek must be," he said; and sure enough, passing through an area of town that seemed to have been bombed, or perhaps ravaged by some form of brick-blight, somewhere down there we found it.

Its waters are not exactly black, because they are thick with floating oil and scum. They are lined with the yards of tanners, and wherever we looked odious effluents seemed to be leaking into the creek. A few barges lay there; across the river we could see, rank upon rank in dingy pageantry, the monuments of the Laurel Hill cemetery; there were belching and thumping noises in the air; far to the west, like a Dantean irony, stood the resplendent tower of the Empire State Building, in another world. A man who joined us there, wiping his hands on a grease rag, was full of mordant information about the Newtown Creek. You couldn't swim in it, he said, because it was too thick to move your arms. On the other hand you would never drown, because you couldn't sink. It blistered the paint off the tugboats. It tarnished any brasswork in ten minutes. You couldn't put a fire out with it, there was too much oil. No fish could live in it: only germs and water rats.

And yet, as I said to somebody else in astonishment, returning from this excursion, it really is the *sea*—the sea in Brooklyn. "Thalassa!" he observed without enthusiasm, having seen it for himself.

I was always conscious now of living on the Bay, and began to make the acquaintance of the watermen. In the past New York must have been marvelously rich in harbor people—not only the deep-sea sailormen, but all the leathery company of boatmen, ferrymen, oyster fishers, tugmen, and dredgemen. The oyster beds of New York harbor were celebrated in those days, before pollution poisoned them, and there were dynasties of prosperous oyster families on Staten Island, with comfortable country houses along the shores of the Kill van Kull. Livery boatmen plied all over the city, innumerable ferries crossed the Hudson and the East River, hundreds of New Yorkers fished for a living. Generations of mudlarks looked for sand dollars on the Manhattan shore, or lured the blue crabs from the Harlem River with hunks of meat on strings, to cook and eat them on the bank. The sea was not only the occupation, but the *pre*-occupation of New York. It was to the waterfront that the bourgeoisie strolled, to catch the cool breezes off the Bay, and mingle with the harbor folk. The ocean and its crafts impregnated the whole city. The clipper captains were lions of New York.

Today the presence of the port and its workers is more diffuse. The nearest thing to a sailors' quarter in New York is perhaps the district called Chelsea, between West 14th and 30th Streets, but even it is far better known as a resort of artists and writers, where Dylan Thomas roistered in the Chelsea Hotel, and Clement Clarke Moore wrote " 'Twas the night before Christmas." Most of the longshoremen, stevedores, and seamen live well away from the harbor like everyone else, and this is not a city (like Hamburg, say, or Liverpool) where cafés and pubs are pointed out to you as well-known sailors' favorites. In New York maritime currents do eddy through the daily life of the city, but you must look harder for them. "See that guy there with the bag?" my companion once asked me, as we walked through Harlem in the morning. "I'd like to bet you fifty to one he's got a load of stuff he's lighted down at the docks." On Lenox Avenue, he assured me, nobody need pay the full price for a bottle of whisky, or pine for a twist of cannabis: there was nothing that did not find its way surreptitiously to Harlem, by well-worn tracks from the waterfront. You never know in New York who belongs to the freemasonry of the port. It may be the man with the Lenox Avenue bag, cannily summing up his customers before offering them a Japanese transistor, or it may be the staid and scholarly-looking man beside you on the bus, reading *Jane Eyre,* who turns out to be a harbor pilot fresh from the morning tide.

The seamen themselves blend indistinguishably into megalopolis, except on the street corners around the ship-shaped and portholed headquarters of the National Maritime Union, though there must be several thousand at large in New York any day of the year. Such taverns as there are behind the waterfront, anywhere around the Bay, notably lack the quarterdeck spirit, and seem to be frequented, in my limited and diffident experience, chiefly by solitary melancholics. The seamen's clubs and institutes are scattered all over the city— the Norwegian Seamen's Church in Brooklyn, the British Seamen's Club grandly in Gramercy Park, the Mariners Family Home for Aged Women in Tomkins Avenue on Staten Island. Charitable buses take foreign seamen from Manhattan to play soccer in Port Newark. Hostesses are available, with Club Rooms too, at the Belgian Seamen's Club on Pier 36. The Shrine Church of the Sea, on Eleventh Avenue near 14th Street, offers special prayers for "longshoremen, seamen, truck drivers, and all who labor along our waterfront"—besides supplying Catholic chaplains for ocean-going ships.

There used to be permanent pools of foreign sailors in New York, ready to fill vacancies in the crews of incoming vessels. Now if a seaman is needed he is flown over from Europe, but sailors from all over the world are still to be found at the Seamen's Church Institute near the Battery, at the southern tip of Manhattan, awaiting berths or taking

time off. This is traditionally the meeting place of foreign
mariners in New York. It was financed in the first place by a
group of citizens of such unimaginable wealth that many
radicals assumed it to be a substitute for improving conditions
at sea; but it replaced a whole row of unsavory boardinghouses along South Street, where seamen had often been
shanghaied into service (the practice was born on the West
Coast, but the Oxford Dictionary's first quotation of the
word is from the New York *Tribune,* 1871). The Institute
recently moved into a tidy medium-sized skyscraper, and I
often looked in when I was down in lower Manhattan, for I
liked its brisk flavor, and was entertained to see its brawny
clientele, straight it seemed from the fo'csle, absorbed into
the milieu of air-conditioned bedrooms and modernistic
décor. At the Institute the sailor ashore may not only bank
his money, learn to paint water-colors, or work for his mate's
certificate, but may also pick up his mail—which, as he has
pottered around the trade routes from Penang to Valparaiso,
may have been awaiting him year after year in the port that
every sailor reaches someday.

I doubt if many native New Yorkers go to sea professionally nowadays, unless the Navy makes them, but there
are said to be some 5,600 men who work afloat within the
harbor, on tugs, lighters, ferries, and pilot boats. A few citizens still make their living by fishing, too. In March the shad
fishermen of the Hudson River hang their nets on thickets
of poles—hickory poles fifty or more feet long, which are
staked in rows on the New Jersey side of the stream, to avoid
the ships. During the weeks when the shad are running in
from the sea the fishermen live on barges beside their poles;
their fishing rights are carefully controlled and guarded, and
there is a waiting list for licenses. Other rivermen lay eelpots
in the Hudson—the mouth of the Harlem River is a rich

eel-ground—and a handful of men earns a living by clam digging in the few unpolluted reaches of the Bay, inside the arm of Sandy Hook. I was once flying over the East River when I noticed an armada of what looked like pleasure yachts, steaming line ahead towards Hell Gate, and looking exceedingly trim and comfortable. Yachtsmen's convention, I surmised? Yale, Harvard, and Princeton Sailing Clubs, on a joint excursion into the Sound? No, it was the fishing skippers of Sheepshead Bay, on their way to Gracie Mansion to present a professional grievance to the Mayor.

Sheepshead Bay, on the southern shore of Brooklyn, is now the chief professional fishing harbor of the New York region, and is also a watering place of an old-fashioned razzle-dazzle kind. It has a famous fish restaurant, Lundy's, like a beer hall on the waterfront, where jolly Sunday parties eat enormous fish meals, washed down (I was gratified to find) by a cocktail called the Eton and Harrow Martini. Outside, the big fishing boats are lined up splendidly like so many Admirals' barges, with their radio masts and radar, their sparkling paintwork, and their gay names—*Rebel, Speedy, Atomic,* or *Amberjack III.* They earn their living partly by taking amateurs out fishing, in which capacity they are known as "party boats," and are equipped, as they urgently announce, with cocktail bars and Accommodation for Ladies. At other times their captains fish professionally themselves, the last of the New York deep-sea fishermen. You can buy their catch on the quayside, and sometimes the trays of plaice, cod, or mullet are surmounted by proprietorial placards—"Caught on the Donna M. By Johnny Zambarbi and Crew"—which are blazoned authentically with the old pride of the sea. ("You from England?" one Sheepshead skipper asked me, as I loitered beside his boat. "I was over there in the Navy, looking after the girls.")

Back in Manhattan another old familiar of the waterfront
is the fish-market man. He is to be seen at his best at the
Fulton Fish Market, one of the hoariest New York institutions, which straggles along the harborfront of South Street,
but is inevitably destined one day to be shifted to more
convenient and hygienic quarters. For the moment it thrives
much as it always did, grubbily organic and traditional, and
one of the pleasures of the city is breakfast down there at
Sloppy Louie's or the Paris Dining Rooms, when the market
men crowd in for their coffee with that queer mixture of
obscenity and gentle manners that seems characteristic of
market people everywhere.

Before dawn is the time to go, of course, and as you drive
off the Expressway, just below Brooklyn Bridge, you will
know you are approaching Fulton Street by the bustle, the
violent fish smell, the crouching cats in the gutters, and the
flicker of braziers in the streets. The market stands beside
the water on a cobbled street, with old brownstone buildings
opposite and the black mass of the bridge above. It is a market of the northern seas. The fish it chiefly sells are hard
northern fish, slabs of cod, cold-water tunny, flatfish, herring
—tough fish, to be slapped here and there, picked up with
spikes, swung around by their tails, sent skidding along
slippery scrubbed boards—fish that is best stewed, boiled,
jollied along into fish and chips or apotheosized into chowder.
The fish dealers, grumpy-faced in their oilskins beneath the
bare electric lights, are marvelously New York, with names
like Caleb Haley, Solomon Rubenstein, or R. J. Cornelius
Inc., and they exchange pithy scurrilities with each other
over the din of the market, savoring each snub as though it
is a shining aphorism, and sometimes repeating it slowly for
the benefit of bystanders. Sturdy market women are to be
seen doing horrible things to slabs of pinkish tunny, and

through the open doors you may see one or two small fishing
boats, hung with pots and nets, gently undulating with the
East River tide.

It is true that nearly all the fish comes here not by boat at
all, but by refrigerated truck (partly because a gradual rise
in the New York water temperature has driven fish northward to cooler seas). Most of it is from the big New England
fishing ports; you may also find red mullet from Florida
waters, Carolina swordfish, or even a few genuine exotica like
squibs or sea urchins, destined for the more fastidious United
Nations delegations, perhaps, or the fancier *genre* restaurants.
All the same, nothing proclaims the maritimeness of New
York more gloriously than its colossal consumption of fish.
The soft-shell crabs between bread rolls, the fried or stewed
oysters, the Giant Lobsters—all these, steaming or slobbering
in their daily millions, glistening in the shell or all too often
smothered in scarlet sauces, are the city's most constant reminder that the sea is close. Most of all I used to marvel at
the inescapability of clams. Edible clams are almost unknown
in Europe, just as cockles are not eaten in America; but
sometimes New York seems besotted with them. Clam shells
made the wampum that was the currency of the original
Indians; clam chowder remains, to my mind, the supreme
gastronomic specialty of the Eastern seaboard. There is no
more pregnant announcement in New York than the sign on
the diner window, STEAMERS TODAY, and any evening of any
day you may be sure that half a million New Yorkers, from
the Plaza to Joe's Clam Kitchen, are wading into the cherry-
stones, the little necks, or the quahogs (all, as it happens,
venus mercenaria, in different stages of growth). It makes
the mind boggle. What generations of clams, what dynasties,
must be scraped from the sea each day to supply this metropolis, to stock the clam bars and the clam stalls, to give
substance to the Manhattan chowders, to provide that absolute

sine qua non of any self-respecting New York menu, Clams
on the Half Shell!

It is said that a quarter of all the inhabitants of New York
are directly or indirectly supported by the port—by which
the port's publicity men mean, in effect, that if the port did
not exist, nor would New York. Most New Yorkers ignore
this truth, but a fanatic minority, I presently discovered,
thinks of little else. Buffs of many colors now took me in
hand: railway enthusiasts, marine historians, seafood connoisseurs, people who knew all about tugs, or were passionately
concerned with the preservation of South Street, or vehe-
mently dedicated to the restoration of paddle steamers, or in
love with Brooklyn Navy Yard. I met Joseph Mitchell of the
New Yorker, the author of an enchanting book about the
bottom of the harbor, called *The Bottom of the Harbor,* and
Frank Braynard, the marine artist and author, whose attic
contains two thousand pictures of passenger liners, and whose
cellar is equipped with eleven enormous cabinets full of
documents like deck plans and the menus of first-class dining
saloons. I discovered a society dedicated exclusively to the
contemplation of the liner *Titanic,* which has its chairman
and its committee, its annual dinners and I dare say its club
tie. I was invited to India House, a club for shipping people
which is a very shrine of nautophilia, as polished and spanking as a ship itself—ship prints on all its walls, ship models
suspended from its ceilings, admirals, captains, and shipowners in plenty, a fine smell of cigars and hard bargains and a
permanent abundance of clams. I was taken one Sunday to
see a schooner race in the harbor, an event organized around
a replica of the yacht *America*—herself built on the East
River. This was fun. Speedboats splashed about, seaplanes
and helicopters buzzed above us, tugs were dressed overall,
the big Staten Island ferry thudded ponderously through the

festivities, the new *America* and her peers swished around the marker buoys, and benignly in the middle of it all stood the Statue of Liberty.

For thousands of New Yorkers take to the boats for pleasure. Any fine day, April to November, the yachtsmen sail in their armadas into the sheltered waters around the Bay—one of the most astonishing sights of the affluent society. It is still smart, of course, to own a boat. In the Hudson River there sometimes lie yachts of legendary luxury ("floor-to-floor wheelhouse carpeting," as a harbor policeman once put it to me), and in the boat basin at the west end of 79th Street movie actors and Greek millionaires often bask in their yachts among Old Masters and young mistresses, rather than subject themselves to the discomforts of a penthouse suite at the Plaza. I was told of a film producer who used his yacht to move about Manhattan, as others might take a taxi: a fellow guest at a dinner party one night, offered a lift home to his apartment a few blocks away, found himself conveyed by sea from the East Side to the West Side of Manhattan, via Battery Point. They are social sailors, no doubt, who invest in the comic notices to be seen in the yacht stores—*Big Wheel House, Gulls and Buoys, This Button Not to Be Operated until Four Feet Under Water.* Many other New York families, though, take their sailing more seriously, and handle their craft with great skill: I doubt if there is another city in the world that could put such a fleet of yachts into the water. There is a good deal of muscle flexing to these enthusiasms, salt spray on sou'westers, the bold marking of charts and the sipping of piping-hot coffee in unnecessary discomfort. I admired the New York yachtsmen, nevertheless, for it seemed to me that they were responding, as best they could, to some old call of the Yankee, some fundamental impulse of New York—a city which

Southward to the Bay: on the left, the East River, with Queensboro, Williamsburg, Manhattan, and Brooklyn bridges

Northward to the Bronx: on the left, the Hudson River,
with George Washington bridge

On the Newtown Creek

The view from Governors Island

sprang, no less marvelously than Venice, direct out of the sea.

Such sights this great Bay has seen! Such grand occasions in the history of navigation! Perhaps Leif's longboat never sailed past Sandy Hook, but here in 1785 the first vessel ever to sail from America to China undeniably put out: the *Empress of China,* 360 tons, a Hudson River packet, carrying letters from the infant Republic to "The most serene, the most puissant, high, illustrious, noble, honourable, venerable, wise and prudent emperors, kings, republics, princes, dukes, earls, barons, lords, burgomasters, counsellors, as also judges, officers, judiciaries and regents of all the good cities and places, whether ecclesiastical or secular"—which seems, one can hear the lading officer saying, to cover it. From here the noblest of the clippers sailed, *Sea Witch, Rainbow,* the fastest and loveliest things afloat, slowly warped out of their South Street berths, meticulously maneuvered past the Battery, and then away like a song down the upper bay, their canvas spreading as they sailed, away through the Narrows to sea—to San Francisco around the Horn, with Forty-Niners crowding the deck rails, to China or Bombay—to Liverpool in 13 days, to Honolulu in 82, at speeds sometimes of 16 or 18 knots, with a zest and daring unequaled on the seas.

Here along the Hudson River, in 1807, chugged the first profitable steamboat ever built, Fulton's *Clermont,* whose engine was made in England, but whose inventor was a proper New Yorker—the son of an Irish immigrant, born on the East Side of Manhattan and buried in Trinity Church. The *Clermont* was built on the East River, but made her first powered voyage from a wharf on the Hudson at the foot of what is now 10th Street. She started reluctantly, giving up after a few moments, but presently shuffled away blowing pine sparks all over the place, billowing smoke, and disappearing upstream with loud clanking noises. We are told that the crews of passing sailing vessels fell to their knees in prayer when this phenomenon appeared, and a farmer upriver fled home to report "the devil on his way to Albany in a sawmill." Another eyewitness said the ship looked "precisely like a backwoods sawmill mounted on a scow and set on fire," but she reached Albany safely anyway, and her inventor, true to his native city, acquired a monopoly of steamboat traffic in New York waters, and is honored in the Fulton Fish Market.

In New York harbor, in 1776, the first submarine attack on a warship was launched—by the American submarine *Turtle*, propelled by a hand-cranked propeller, manned by a single hero, made of oak timbers and shaped very properly like a clam. Standing upright in this weird device, Sergeant Ezra Lee set off from the Battery one dark September night with a gunpowder mine attached to his hull, and a piece of phosphorescent wood to illuminate his compass. He submerged his boat with a foot pump, and came up beside the keel of H.M.S. *Eagle*, anchored off Staten Island; but he failed to attach the explosive to the warship, bravely though he tried all night, and on his way home his compass failed, so that he repeatedly bobbed above the surface to get his bearings. Chased by the British from Governors Island, worn out poor fellow by his peculiar exertions, Lee jettisoned his mine, which exploded in the East River, and cranked the *Turtle* wearily back to Manhattan.

Mr. Edward Robb Ellis, in his book *The Epic of New York*, quotes a British officer as saying of this episode: "The ingenuity of these people is singular in their secret modes of mischief," and singular indeed was another famous warship which made its fighting debut from this harbor. The *Monitor* sailed through the Narrows in March 1862, to tackle the Confederate ironclad *Merrimac*, which had been playing havoc with the Federal warships in Hampton Roads, at the southern end of Chesapeake Bay. There had never been such a ship before: almost unnoticeable in the waters of the Bay, all that showed of her was an iron-plated deck, a few inches above the water, a huge iron gun turret, and the smoke from two almost invisible funnels. This ship was designed by the Swede John Ericsson, now to be seen in effigy clutching a model of her at Battery Point, who had first offered the idea to the Emperor Napoleon III of France. She slipped out to sea painfully that day, for she was brand-new, leaky, and not really an ocean-going vessel at all; but her epic contest with the *Merrimac* three days later, so Winston Churchill judged, "made the greatest change in sea-fighting since cannon fired by gun-powder had been mounted on ships, about four hundred years before."

Most of the greatest passenger steamers of the world made their first voyages into, or out of, this harbor: the *Savannah* sailing one way, the *Great Western* the other, Brunel's enormous *Great Eastern* scraping precariously over the Sandy Hook bar, the incomparable yachtlike liners of the Inman Line, the ever faster, ever bigger, ever grander ships that fought for the Atlantic trade in the heyday of the passenger liner. The *Lusitania* sailed from New York, to be torpedoed off Ireland in 1915; the *Normandie,* one of the most splendid liners ever built, was burnt out at Pier 88 in 1942.

What scenes to remember! Most New Yorkers may prefer to let them go, but soon I could see them all in my mind's eye: the blockading warships of the Royal Navy, too, so often tossed about beyond Sandy Hook, and the gray-painted troopships joining their convoys, and the *Queen Elizabeth* sliding out to sea as Mr. Tobin had seen her, and many another sea spectacle of New York, as the tugmen described them to me, or the amateurs of the harbor remembered them in privately printed monographs and after-dinner speeches. All the great ships come to New York. The *Flying Dutch-*

man herself once sailed through the Narrows, in the days of Peter Stuyvesant; when she failed to stop, the gunners of Manhattan fired their cannon at her, but the balls, we are told, "went whistling through her cloudy and imponderable mass."

Chapter 5

IN THE ARCHIPELAGO

I set out next to explore the islands which litter this confluence of sea and river. New York is an archipelago, like Venice, a clutter of islands, large and small, of which Manhattan forms the glittering centerpiece. As the Venetians chose as their headquarters the central island of Saint Mark's, so the original settlers of Manhattan went to Manhattan because it was in the middle—easily defensible, commanding, accessible. I soon came to realize how much easier life is in a land city, even one so sprawling as London, for even now the island nature of New York makes it laborious to move from one part of the city to another: one has to make for a bridge, one has to pay for a tunnel, one has to wait for a ferry, or one just gives up, and confines oneself to looking at Brooklyn from the opposite shore, or postponing Weehawken yet again. To New Yorkers it is only a fact of life: to most of them Manhattan *is* the city, and the rest of the Bay shore is separate territory—"I live out of the city," they say, "in Queens." But I suspect the need to hop from island to island inside the city limits, like the Indians "going from one part to another," has powerfully contributed to New York's inherited sense of motion, and its always unsettled tastes.

Two of the islands, Long Island and Staten Island, are so big as to be scarcely considered islands at all, and really form part of the land mass around the Bay. On many others the New Yorkers long ago decided that they would deposit their unwanted institutions, to get them out of sight and mind. The British kept their convicts on hulks in the Bay. The Americans dispatched their criminals, their lunatics, their incurables, even just their poor and aged, to the less attractive blobs on the harbor chart.

One of the gloomiest places I know in the world is Welfare Island, familiar from a distance to every New Yorker, which lies in the East River between 50th and 86th Streets. The Queensboro Bridge strides high above it, and is connected with the island by a big brown tower, like a blocktower, which contains an elevator. Though one can in fact drive onto Welfare Island by a lesser bridge from Queens, this froward edifice set the tone of the island for me, and made me think it was accessible only by chains and pulleys, as you might be lowered into a pit. The bridge casts a shadow over the place, moreover, and high above the island the traffic relentlessly rumbles: it is like looking up to the sunny street through a basement grille.

Welfare Island accordingly has a downtrodden air, and along its narrow length colorless buildings, some apparently abandoned, some showing feeble signs of survival, breathe the institutional spirit. Incurable old ladies live on Welfare Island, and the New York Fire Department has a training center there, trailing hoses and dribbling foam all over the place. Attendants in white coats emerge from a building near the eastern bank in which several hundred doomed monkeys await, in hygienic cages, the attentions of New York University scientists. I never discovered what all the other buildings were, and the few people I met walking about those weedy roadways, paroled patients, perhaps, or refugees from some unmentionable establishment beyond, seemed to answer my questions evasively, as though they had been brainwashed. Welfare Island is one of those places, familiar to every great city, whose future has been in the air as long as anyone can remember, and is periodically discussed in cross editorials, and raised by outraged councilors; but its misery seemed to me permanently embedded there, as though rose gardens or honeymoon bowers could not clear the soil.

There is a poor people's hospital on Ward's Island, upstream in the East River, beneath another pair of bridges; sometimes I used to go to the gardens there, to watch the passing water traffic at Hell Gate, and as the tugs and motorboats foamed past me, as the seagulls wheeled above, as the diesel trains streamed over one bridge, and the cars over another, with all that intensity of purpose that is the hallmark of New York—then sometimes I would turn away from the river, and looking through the iron-mesh fence that surrounds the hospital grounds, in the distance I would see pairs of listless patients walking slowly across the grass in dressing gowns, and frail old ladies in wheel chairs bent over by bored relatives.

On Riker's Island, marvelously set at the head of the East River, where it breaks out into the Sound, they have deposited the city prison ("Correctional Institution for Men"). On North Brothers Island, nearby, there is an infectious diseases hospital. On Hart Island, out in the Sound, there is a narcotics' reform center, and there too the paupers, the miscarried babies, the unidentified corpses, and the amputated limbs of New York are buried, twice a week.

Then in somber ceremonial a party of convicts from the jail, with a truckful of pine coffins, crosses on the little ferry. Silently they drive away to the wind-swept grassy hillock at the north end of the island, where a white obelisk, all alone

on the skyline, stands memorial to all the unknown Jews and
Christians buried there. A trench is dug for those plain
caskets, every Tuesday and Thursday morning, and there
they are left, a hundred and fifty to a trench, marked only
by a numbered stone, until fifteen or twenty years later
they are dug up again to make room for new arrivals; and
by then, I am told, the convicts generally find nothing left
but a few white bones, to mark so many unremembered
tragedies.

Every now and then the New Yorkers take a fresh look at
their islands, and conclude what a waste it all is, in this most
urban of cities, to let such places go to waste. Sometimes they
even translate the sentiment into action, and beautify some
lesser inlet. There is a rock called Mill Rock, just off Gracie
Mansion, which seemed to me one day to be showing signs of
such regeneration, and I asked a passing citizen what was happening. "Nothin'," he replied, "they're just fixin' it up with
trees or grass or sump'n, justa make it look nice, justa keep
the Mayor sweet, that's all." (He was wrong: Park Com-
missioner Moses had done it, just to keep the city sweet.)
A visionary civic benefactor has even installed an ornamental
fountain at the tip of Welfare Island, as if to drown its sor-
rows in spray. There is an island I would like to take in hand
myself. It is called Hoffman Island, was once a seaman's training school, and is now uninhabited; but it lies a mile outside
the Narrows, just beside the shipping channel, and seen there
in the glistening ocean among the ships, with its old laundry
chimney like a campanile in the lagoon, it takes me in spirit
like a swallow to Venice, and makes me wish I owned it.

Some of the New York islands are already islands of delight. Coney Island, indeed, which is really a kind of demi-
island hooked to the Brooklyn shore, was once the most
famous pleasure isle of all. It is no longer what it was, and

nowadays spins its great wheel, shoots its air rifles, and licks its candy floss with less than utter abandon, if only because they are always threatening to close its amusement park altogether, and build apartments all over it. It is a bad place for violence, too. Still, it was Coney Island that Maxim Gorky, of all people, once described as "fabulous beyond conceiving, ineffably beautiful . . . this fiery scintillation"; and for anyone over thirty-five in the English-speaking world it remains the synonym of spree, a folk memory from the years of honky-tonk, the Big Band, and the DC-3.

City Island, at the other end of New York, is a jolly sportsman's island. I admired a succinct sign I saw there once: "Fishing Persons Only." It lies at the entrance to the Sound, off the Bronx, and is covered all over with boatyards, sail lofts, chandlers, and yacht provisioners. It was once a whaling base—in the eighteenth and early nineteenth centuries many whales were harpooned in the Sound—and is still the home of some celebrated yacht riggers and sailmakers, including the firm that made the sails for the original *America*. For the most part, though, it is boisterously amateur: if South Street once stood for New York's supreme professionalism at sea, City Island now means, to many a maritime purist, the vulgarity of ill-navigated ostentatious launches, and the boom of transistor radios on summer nights, reverberating to the clink of glasses through the marshy inlets of the Sound.

The most agreeably surprising of the islands is Governors Island, a few hundred yards off Battery Point, at the southern tip of Manhattan. This was the site of the very first European settlement in New York: the original party of pioneers from Holland camped here before they ventured on to Manhattan. They called it Nut Island. Later it became the military headquarters of New York, first British, then American, and it is now the regional base of the United States Coast Guard. It is about a mile square, and a private ferry links it with the Battery.

There is no more astonishing contrast in New York, than the one which this short voyage provides. A Coast Guard sentry greets you when you disembark, saluting you with the odd wringing gesture that is peculiar to United States mariners, as though he wishes he could shake his hand off altogether in the excess of his loyalty. Immediately before you is the rampart of an old fort, and a short walk up an incline brings you to an exquisite green sward, like an old Southern campus, or perhaps a theological retreat. Handsome official residences, one or two of them Colonial, line this unexpected mall, with white balconies in front, and gardens behind overlooking the Buttermilk Channel and the Brooklyn shore; rows of fine elms march away to the far end, where you may dimly discern, as in a dream, the spire of a sweetly rural church. Nowhere in New York feels more pastoral: but immediately behind you, so close you may imagine the clatter of the ticker tapes, the ringing of the telephones, the hiss of the elevators, the great mass of the downtown skyscrapers, tower by tower, peers down upon you like Big Brother.

In old pictures of New York Bedloe's Island does not look much—just a flattish islet in the upper bay with a fort upon it. It was one of the harbor's defensive stations, and had been ceded for this reason by the State of New York to the Federal Government, having gone through the conventional New York cycle of quarantine station, pesthouse, and isolation camp. It might have remained in obscurity were it not for the fact that in 1875 a group of Frenchmen decided to present to the Americans a token of respect for their country, in the shape of that substantial female figure whose nose we hovered about near the beginning of this book. The Americans, raising the necessary cash with extreme difficulty, agreed to provide the pedestal, if the French would provide the lady. Fortunately, the polygonal fort upon the island provided a ready-made foundation, and after ten years of exhortation, reproach, and newspaper campaigning the site was prepared at last, the statue sailed in recumbent upon a French freighter, and the memorial to Liberty was erected. Today the island is renamed Liberty Island in her honor.

Her fine bosomy figure, a true emblem of New York's stature, if not its character, was the creation of Frédéric Bartholdi, sculptor of the Lion of Belfort. The iron framework of the statue was the work of Gustave Eiffel, of the Eiffel Tower, and the torch in the lady's hand was redesigned in 1916 by Gutzon Borglum, the man who cut the colossal faces of the American Presidents in the flank of Mount Rushmore. There could hardly be a finer site for the Statue of Liberty, and it is not easy in New York to escape her matronly benediction. Like the headmaster's wife at the beginning of term, she greets you inexorably as you sail in through the harbor, and keeps her eye on you throughout: there are many places in the mainland round about, far away in Brooklyn or New Jersey, where you may see her torso protruding above the landscapes in back view or in profile. At night she is illuminated; in the daytime ferryboats constantly pester her, summer and winter, with the tourists they deposit at her feet.

I went to Liberty Island one day with an Australian acquaintance, passing through New York on his way home to Tasmania. He did not think much of the statue, and said it reminded him of Russia. I suppose its romantic symbolism has lost much of its appeal nowadays, and certainly the pilgrims to the island are not always respectful, as the entries in the visitors' book show—"A fine place to visit but I wouldn't want to live there," "I plead the Fifth Amendment," "Spooky Stairways," "It leaks," "Give it back to the French."

I have doubts, too, about the visitor who wrote "Inspirational," and signed himself "Yaga Booga, Huflong, Mongolia." But though I sympathize with the lady who thought it was a "nice sight but the Stairs weren't that wide," still I am myself easily moved by the Statue of Liberty. It may not be great art, but it is spectacular engineering still—one of the most colossal sculptures, as the guidebook says with pardonable rodomontade, in the history of the world. The lady's nose is 4½ feet long, her fingernail is 13 by 10 inches, her mouth is three feet wide, and her waist is 35 feet around. Few people observe the date (July 4, 1776) on the plaque she holds in her left hand, and only privileged sightseers in helicopters can see the broken shackle—British made, I fear—which protrudes from the hem of her Grecian skirt.

Too bloody big, my Australian thought, and it is easy to sneer. Upon the pedestal are inscribed Emma Lazarus's famous lines:

> *Give me your tired, your poor,*
> *Your huddled masses yearning to breathe free,*
> *The wretched refuse of your teeming shore . . .*

But even these are not so well regarded as they used to be, for they are considered scarcely polite to such friendly states as Italy, Ireland, or Soviet Russia, from whose teeming shores that refuse came; when they were reproduced upon a slab at Kennedy Airport the refuse reference was tactfully omitted, to the annoyance of literary commentators. The poem still pleases me, though, and for me there remains a touching nobility to that tremendous figure, raising her lamp beside the golden door. So many newcomers have felt their hearts lift, to see her waiting there, and so many Americans have watched her with a pang, as their ships sailed out through the Narrows to the sea, and that inflexible spinster,

smaller and smaller against the skyline, stood there in the
harbor like an image of home and certainty.

Liberty Island is poignant in one way: the next island
across the water is poignant in quite another. It is scarcely
a stone's throw from the statue, but it is haunted by still
more disillusioned spirits.

Long ago it was the center of a profitable oyster bed, and
it was known to the Dutch as Oyster Island. The English,
in their cheerful way, found it a convenient place for string-
ing up unsuccessful pirates, and called it Gibbet Island; the
Americans agreed, and in 1831, we read, a vast and enthusi-
astic crowd of New Yorkers, in steamboats, yachts, schooners,
and canoes, loitered around the island limits when two
particularly notorious buccaneers were hanged. For years it
was a recruiting depot. ("Wanted," says a proclamation
concerning a volunteer who changed his mind, and fled the
island, "Thomas Fyne of the Corps of Artillerists and Engineers, five foot six inches, of a dark complexion, slovenly
habit, and indolent deportment"—just the man the Army
needed.) The island was gradually enlarged in the nineteenth
century, mostly by the dumping of ballast from foreign
ships, and upon this cosmopolitan foundation there was
established, in 1894, the most celebrated of all the immigration
stations of history: Ellis Island.

They built it, so they say, in the Renaissance style—or at
least, as one official publication put it at the time, the
Renaissance style "was accentuated over other kinds of architecture." In fact it looked like a cross between a workhouse,
a railway depot, and a peculiarly forbidding, but not in-
expensive, girls' boarding school. It had pretensions to
grandeur, with towers, a monumental entrance, and its own
ferry slip, and it was entirely self-contained, generating its

own power, pumping its own water, with its own laundries, hospitals, and steam-operated heating plants. It was built of a gray foreboding granite, and sat rather squatly upon the water, filling almost the whole expanse of the island.

Through this uninviting place, between 1897 and 1954, 16 million immigrants passed—the entire population of contemporary Yugoslavia, say, or twice the population of the city of New York. They were taken there in barges direct from incoming ships, and subjected to a brisk and fateful examination. If they passed, presently they became Americans. If they failed, back they went to the barges, the ships, and the slums of Europe—for it was only steerage-class passengers who were welcomed in this way, wealthier immigrants going through the formalities on board their ships.

In they came, those multitudes of Russians, Italians, Scandinavians, Jews, pouring into Ellis Island, barge after bargeload down the decades. In the Grand Hall they were lined up for a medical examination. The line took a right-angled turn at the first doctor's desk, so that an alien could be examined, like a bull, front face, side view, and from the back, where spinal deformities would show. The second doctor looked only at eyes, for trachoma. If there was anything apparently wrong with a man, they chalked a white cross upon his clothing, and sent him elsewhere for a closer check. Otherwise he shuffled on to an aptitude test—thirty-eight questions in two minutes, fired at him very fast out of the blue, with a reading test of a Biblical extract in any language.

It was all done at breakneck speed, and the immigrants, who had only that very hour arrived in the New World, must have been cruelly bewildered by the hustled impersonality of it all. The vast majority got safely through nevertheless. Those who failed the tests were either remanded to the grim dormitories of Ellis Island, waiting for a higher decision, or else, wham, within the hour they were on their way back to the ships, the dreams of lifetimes, and very likely the savings too, shattered after one tantalizing glimpse of the Manhattan skyline. There is a heart-rending movie of one such batch of discards, taken I would imagine in the early twenties. They emerge from the portals of the Grand Hall in a black, sad, tattered mass, and they move in procession towards the barges. Two immigration officers, in mustaches and long greatcoats, are ushering them ingratiatingly, it seems, towards the landing stage, and one is irresistibly reminded of rich country gentlemen glad to be seeing the last of uninvited poor relations. *"Bon voyage!"* one can almost hear them saying, "Sorry you can't stay longer!"—and as the rejects of America re-embark, the camera catches for a moment the face of a pale boy in the front of the crowd. He is a hunchback, hobbling with difficulty towards the quay with a crutch and a bag of possessions, and there is upon his face an expression of indescribable despair. What became of him, I wonder? Did Auschwitz or Belsen welcome him instead?

Most immigrants were through Ellis Island in a couple of hours, and proceeded in barges to the New Jersey shore, or by ferry steamer to Manhattan. The fate of the minority, lingering on through appeal and disputation on the island, or instantly rejected, has long disturbed American consciences, and has given the name of Ellis Island a disturbing endorsement. The unmistakable silhouette of the island has a meaning for every New Yorker. Though in fact it played its historic role for only half a century, nearly every Italian, Polish, German, or Russian American one meets claims that his grandfather or great-grandfather came through Ellis Island —an earthier, and rather more convincing, parallel to the claim that one's forebears came over, or were even born, upon the *Mayflower*.

The island is empty now, looked after by the National Parks Commission, and destined one day, they say, to become a memorial to all the immigrants. I went there once by helicopter, landing on an overgrown playing field, and being met there by a warden in a wide-brimmed hat, like Boy Scouts long ago, or doughboys. He came over most days, he told me, in his outboard motorboat from Liberty Island, and together he and I tramped through the deserted halls: the grandiose saloon where they lined up for those doctors; the cheerless dormitories (hosed down in those days, the warden told me, regularly from floor to ceiling); the family room where, twice a week, husbands, wives, and children were reunited, looking out together through wire-meshed windows to the Wall Street towers across the water; the lawyers' consultation room—many lawyers made a profession out of Ellis Island, and the legal tangles of immigration provided the foundation of several flourishing New York law firms.

Here we found the remains of a library, stocked mostly with books of Christian Science; and spilled over toppled desks, bulging from broken cupboards, was a mass of bureaucratic paraphernalia, the duplicate forms and labels and lists and pro formas by which those 16 million souls were sorted, labeled, and classified. Far down in the basement, among the heating pipes, a row of barred cells with iron beds seemed to hold the caged ghosts of recalcitrant Slavs. There was a visiting room, where detainees might talk to visitors through a grille, and a currency exchange bank, across whose counters must have passed unimaginable computations of zlotys, sucres, or rubles. In a half-opened drawer I found a pile of language cards, and took one when the warden was not looking. It was a Dutch reading test, and its text in translation was ironically apt: "This our bread we took hot for our provision out of our houses on the day we came forth to go unto you: but now, behold, it is dry, and it is mouldy."

Sometimes they had tried to cheer the place up, and during the Depression artists of the Federal Arts Project embellished a few rooms with symbolic murals, glorifying the unity of the peoples, and portraying immigrants of lofty mien in attitudes of unvarying diligence—"that's an Irishman for sure," said my companion, pointing to a laborer of saintly sobriety. The recreation room had been touched up here and there with bright paint, long since faded, though it was colored for me by the reply of a woman immigrant who was asked how she spent her time in the room, during her twice-weekly couple of hours with her husband: "Crying, mostly."

All in all, with its barbed wire and its half-sunken ferry-boat at the slip, the poison ivy that crawls outside, the sea mist which, in the winter months, hangs perpetually in its corridors, Ellis Island is a very somber place. One forgets that it was a place of fulfillment, as well as disillusion. Only one room seemed to me to be animated by a happier spirit. On my word of honor, I did not have to be told which was the room in which successful immigrants heard the good news of their acceptance, and assembled their bags and families for the triumphant last voyage ashore. It was no more cheerfully decorated than any other room on the island, but some old evocation of hope and vivacity sprang from its boards, and made America feel a grand excitement still.

Certainly nobody will deny excitement to the last of the New York islands, the centerpiece of Bay and archipelago, the hub of this place of movement—Manhattan. For this kaleidoscopic island my imagery, I discovered, shifted mood by mood, or light by light. It is an island of savagery, and sometimes seemed to me to crouch there viciously in its Bay. But it is a highly cultivated island too, and shines often with an air of grace, Bach-like in its geometric splendor, Mendelssohnian in the spring. In the evening once, when I swung away from the island in a helicopter, as the lights sprang up in the skyscraper forest, and the chains of the great bridges were illuminated, the tears came to my eyes to consider all the fears, anxieties, and disillusionments that hung about that city.

And sometimes, from a boat especially, it seemed to me that Manhattan had a dowager look. This *grande dame* is young no longer, for all her energy, and she has seen life in the raw, and she has watched the great Bay come to life down the centuries, to spread its wealth and bustle ever further from the harbor. Sometimes Manhattan has a positively upstage air, as though slightly affronted by the noise, and then she looks out across the harbor as out of a grandstand —lorgnettish, erect, even leaning defensively backward.

All around her she sees the blast, the color, the ceaseless vulgar rumpus of the port.

Two

FUNCTIONAL

Chapter 6

ELEMENTS

When I thought I had the hang of the harbor, its islands, bays, and waterways, I set out to see how it worked. I was determined to educate that man in the subway, if ever I bumped into him again. "What's it to me?" he had demanded, and I wanted to be able to tell him. Sometimes I met Mr. Tobin, and he arranged introductions for me, and told me of new developments; and from his office a constant flow of literature reached me, assuring me of the size and splendor of the port.

Officially its center is the Statue of Liberty —40°41′ North, 74°2′ West. The port district extends to a radius of 25 miles from the statue, in the States of New York and New Jersey, and includes more than 750 miles of water frontage, three major airports, three heliports, and the termini of eight trunk railroads, at least two of them bankrupt. Some 3,000 tugs, lighters, and car floats chug about this complex, and the whole is linked by some of the world's most impressive bridges, one of the world's most elaborate highway systems, several of the world's busiest tunnels, and the world's worst subway.

The sea is New York's first element, and every forty

minutes or so, on average through the year, a ship approaches
the port out of the Atlantic. The mariner's first welcome is
the Ambrose Light, mounted on a tower at the entrance to
the lower bay, off Sandy Hook, and flashing (so my pilot
guide tells me) Gp. Fl. W7. 5. This is a very modern aid
to navigation, replacing in 1967 a lightship posted to some
less spectacular station. It is a steel stilted tower with a
helicopter pad, in which five men of the United States Coast
Guard spend agreeable tours of duty, sustained by air-
conditioning, deep freezers of meat and fish, color television,
radios all over the place, fishing rods provided by the service,
and a reproduction Renoir on a wall. Flags stream gaily from
the tower, and on a fine day it is a marvelous place to watch
the ships go by, in procession towards New York. Better still,
though, is its distant view of the mainland. There the sea
and the low line of the shore seem to blend, the houses on
the Rockaway shore dance in haze and surf, and far in the
distance, twenty miles across the flatlands of Long Island, the
skyscrapers stand white against the sky.

This is a first announcement of New York, a thrilling
hint of what lies through the Narrows. Again I am reminded
of Venice, with St. Mark's theatrically sighted from the
Chioggia channel, high above the mudbanks of the lagoon.
Like Venice, New York is a secret kind of landfall, hidden
within its water gate, and seeming to wait there like a
treasure house for tribute out of the sea. As ports go it is
not easy to approach. The entrance to the Bay is protected
by Sandy Hook, a spit of land five miles long which is usually
regarded as the outer limit of the harbor, and means home
and dry in mariner's parlance. This narrows the harbor
entrance to six miles of what looks like open water, but in
fact a sandbar runs from one shore to the other. It is very
close to the surface in places, and in *The Bottom of the
Harbor* Mr. Mitchell tells the story of a man who wanted

to put on a top hat and stand waist-deep on one of its bumps, waving to the passengers on the *Queen Elizabeth* as they passed stupefied towards the port. By the Ambrose Light the ships accordingly pick up a pilot, and are guided along the deeply dredged Ambrose Channel into the Narrows.

In the past the existence of the Sandy Hook bar threatened to cripple New York as a port: rivals in Boston and Philadelphia hoped it would. It is made of shifty sea sand, not of alluvial deposits from the Hudson, and sometimes seemed likely to block the ship channel altogether. Ships often went aground, and when the *Great Eastern*, then the largest ship ever built, sailed into New York for the first time in 1860, she scraped so barely over the bar that some observers claimed she actually touched bottom—"though among those cognizant of the fact," the *Herald* reported next day, perhaps anxious for its own livelihood, "it was generally agreed that the discolored water which marked the spot was only the stirring up of the great deep by her screw."

Another difficulty used to be the New York tides, which are not especially deep, but are peculiar. They are caused by the double sea entrance—from the south through Sandy Hook, from the north through Long Island Sound. Hell Gate, where the tides more or less meet, is 22½ miles from the open sea by the southern route, but 100 miles by the northern route: this means that there is three hours' difference between high tides at the two ends of the East River—awkward in sailing-ship days, when the East River piers were the fulcrum of the port. There is a sizable difference in tide levels, too, in different parts of the port, and a complicated pattern of currents is swished about by these varying pressures of the sea.

But currents are no longer much hazard. Once past Sandy Hook the steamship captain is in waters as safe as any: only an occasional venturesome yachtsman, treading a cautious

way past Hell Gate, feels the fury of the tides in the old way.
New York's advantages as a port far outweigh her demerits,
and have long given her the edge over her rivals—Boston,
Philadelphia, New Orleans, Norfolk, Portland, Charleston,
Baltimore, or Savannah. Safe anchorage is one, freedom from
fog another: the sea fogs which sometimes lie thick about
the Ambrose Light, and set the foghorns anxiously bellowing,
seldom penetrate the Narrows for long, or lie very thickly
over the inner harbor.

The double sea entrance, via the Bay or via the Sound,
gave the port many advantages during its developing period.
In bad weather captains could give themselves an extra
hundred miles of sheltered passage if they came the back
way; there can seldom have been a day, in the whole history
of this port, when no ship made landfall in New York. In
wartime ships could conveniently slip out by the northern
route, if Sandy Hook was blockaded, and in peacetime all
the considerable coastal trade with New England could comfortably go that way—some 3 per cent of New York's sea
traffic still does. The Hudson, of course, gave New York the
advantage of an onward passage far into the American
interior; and the watery nature of the place, complex yet
compact, provided a vast extent of waterfront, all sheltered
and accessible.

New York is handily situated for most of the great trade
routes—to Europe, to South America, to the Mediterranean.
It has maintained links with the Pacific, too, ever since the
Empress of China sailed for Canton: in the 1848 Gold Rush
140 ships left New York for California, round the Horn,
and another 37 dumped their 11,000 passengers on the
Isthmus of Panama, where more than half of them died of
hunger or tropical disease as they straggled towards the
Pacific coast. The opening of the Panama Canal, in 1900,
vastly increased this traffic, and made New York in a real

sense the central port of the world. Today it is pre-eminently a port of foreign trade. Two-thirds of the ships that use this harbor are coming or going from foreign parts, and if you go by value well over a third of all American imports and exports are handled here. The greatest source of imports (not counting bulk cargoes like ore and oil) is Europe, followed by the Far East and Latin America. The chief destination for exports is the Far East, with Europe not far behind and Latin America a laggard third. In 1967 the total value of this city's foreign trade was $12.8 billion; in the same year the total overseas trade of the Kingdom of Sweden was worth $9.2 billion. I was told once that a third of all the things, animate or inanimate, that have ever arrived at or departed from the United States have passed through the port of New York.

In the old days the mass of New York shipping generally made its way through the upper bay to the East River, where it docked in the long line of piers fronting South Street, and was joined by the traffic entering New York from the Sound. The streets of the lower East Side of Manhattan formed in those days a proper dockland, with all the orthodox grogshops, brothels, and boardinghouses. Here lived the crimps, who earned their living by guiding particularly drunken sailors back to their ships, and a whole community of bargees, thieves, and layabouts resided in and around the piers, sometimes setting up home actually within the great creaking piles of the wharves. In the winter fleets of barges were laid up there, their crews and their families living on board, and the Seamen's Church Institute had a curious floating church moored to a pier, with a steeple. Above the whole scene, looming across South Street, were the great bowsprits of the sailing ships, and the towering filigrees of their masts and rigging.

Today few ships use the South Street piers, which are mostly dilapidated, though there does still linger in those parts a half-imaginary odor of tar, rope, and rum. It is there that the enthusiasts are trying to make their maritime museum, and I spent many agreeable hours wandering around the old brown merchants' houses, loitering in the purlieus of the fish market, or sitting on rickety wharves watching the tugs go by. As ships got bigger, and as steam came in, there was a shift of activity to the Hudson, on the other side of Manhattan. The early steamers often made fools of themselves threshing about the narrow East River, and when the Cunard Steamship Company built a pier on the New Jersey side of the Hudson they set a trend that was soon followed. The decline of South Street began, and will soon reach its nadir with the removal of the Fulton Fish Market and the demolition of nearly everything else.

Most of the big ocean companies then established themselves upon the Hudson, and by the start of the twentieth century the lower West Side of Manhattan was tasseled with that long line of finger piers, protruding at right angles into the river, which is to most people the port of New York. The passenger lines mostly set up their termini in mid-Manhattan, within taxi distance of the city center, and soon one of the traditional sights of New York was the parade of great liners which lay always at the North River piers, side by side, dwarfing the pier buildings with their high smokestacks, and powerfully reinforcing the sensation that everything sleek, rich, and formidable was migrating to New York.

But by the end of the Second World War the Manhattan piers, too, were past their best. They were depressed by labor troubles, congestion in the streets behind, the decline of passenger traffic. Many of them are now derelict, their grandiose wooden towers falling apart at the planks, or slowly leaning outwards into the water. Even those still in use have a melancholy, dingy air, as though they are members of a dying port, and when I was there I never saw a sadder harborfront than those cold neglected piers where the Ocean Greyhounds moored. Like everything else in New York, this will soon change, for the Port of New York Authority is about to build a glittering new passenger terminal in those parts, to serve all the steamship lines, and to incorporate all the lessons learnt in other ports during the past half-century or so; but even this will be less a sign of revival than of changed function, for nothing will bring back the transatlantic liner traffic, and most of the ships using these splendid premises will not be instruments of transport at all, but only floating palaces of entertainment.

For the real impetus of the port has shifted again, so that nowadays most of the New York cargo tonnage never touches Manhattan. Once past Sandy Hook, that procession of shipping abruptly disperses, and disappears into basins, straits, and inlets all over the Bay. Almost anywhere in the archipelago you may find a ship, or at least a barge, being worked: discharging oil in the Arthur Kill, passing through the swing bridge out of Eastchester Bay into the Hutchinson River, plodding up to Spuyten Duyvil beside the expressways, dejectedly unloading coal in the Newtown Creek.

The map of New York is crenelated with piers and docks. There are docks all the way down the Bayonne shore, to the Kill van Kull that separates it from Staten Island. There is a great complex of docks at Brooklyn. There are piers along the Staten Island shore of the Narrows. There are half a dozen piers at Perth Amboy, and all along the Arthur Kill into Newark Bay are jetties for tankers and freighters. Newark Bay itself is a huge land-enclosed stretch of water at the mouths of the Passaic and Hackensack Rivers, lying parallel to the upper bay of New York, and separated from it by the peninsula of Bayonne; upon its shores there is another complete system of docks, Port Newark, and the spectacular brand-new Port Elizabeth, which is to many a foreign seaman the true waterfront of New York. All these separate installations form part of the port of New York, a leviathan among seaports, and outranked in the world only by that port of all Europe, Rotterdam.

Some of them are themselves substantial ports in their own right, big enough to be the principal international harbors of many a less expansive republic. Together they offer more than 200 piers, enough to berth at any one moment 400 ocean-going vessels—the entire Norwegian merchant fleet, say, which is the third largest in the world. This scattered complexity has not always made New York an easy place to run. As I was later to discover, it has often been hamstrung by inner rivalries—at one particular moment of despair, I was told, they thought of abandoning New York Bay altogether, and dredging an entirely new port in the marshes of Jamaica Bay. But the diffuse nature of the port also makes for accessibility. No ship has far to sail. There is no dreary up-river haul to New York, such as delays the impatient voyager to London, Hamburg, or Philadelphia. New York is a squarish shape of seaport, all its corners close to the sea.

The port's second element is the air. The skies of New York are almost never silent or still, and on a fine day they seem to be alive with the streaks of the jets. Aesthetically the air age suits the place: its vast brilliant skies receive the vapor trails like canvases before the brush of an abstractionist, and the svelte forms of the jets complement its architecture. New York is the only great city I know where these machines look altogether at home—not intrusive, nor anachronistic, nor impertinent, nor even remarkable.

But then aircraft and New York go naturally together.

Just as American citizens grew accustomed to the automobile thirty years before the Europeans, so New York was an experienced air terminal at a time when most other cities were flocking to the flying displays. I was taken one day to see the Marine Terminal at La Guardia, from which, between 1940 and 1947, Pan American operated their Clipper flying-boats (Boeing 314s) to the Azores and Lisbon. This is a marvelously evocative place. La Guardia, which stands on the water's edge at the top end of the East River, was the first really modern passenger airport—the first to have beauty shops and drugstores and banks, the first to have grandiose passenger lounges, the first to keep you hanging around in overheated overfed misery in the small hours, waiting for your delayed flight.

Most of it has long been rebuilt, and it is now, to my mind, one of the most civilized of all air terminals, logical, elegant, and comprehensible. The Clipper terminal miraculously survives, and is used for private flying. Outside are the remains of the flying-boat slips, and the narrow jetty by which one boarded the aircraft; the passenger building is circular and chromium-plated, like an old cinema foyer. I had seen pictures of the opening of La Guardia Airport, by Mayor La Guardia himself, in 1939: the scores of DC-3s lined up on the semicircular tarmac, the brass band, the propeller-decked dais, the policemen in their high buttoned jackets, the snap-brimmed photographers, the stewardess, in a pageboy bob and a floral corsage, stepping from the first scheduled flight to arrive—Transcontinental and Western Air from Chicago. In the terminal building all this came to life for me. I heard for myself the throb of the Clipper's engines (four Wright Cyclones), watched the intrepid passengers walk in their fox furs and fedoras down the jetty (only nine of them on the inaugural flight), and thrilled to Pan Am's publicity posters—"Huge 17-ton aerial giants, driven with more horsepower than a locomotive! Giant liners of the sky, speeding from continent to continent in a few incredible hours, overcoming with amazing ease the barriers of distance!" It was from here that Pan Am established the mastery of the Atlantic routes that it has held ever since. Its founder, Juan Trippe, still lived in New York when I was there, and was still its chairman; yet that Clipper terminal already seemed as quaint a period piece as South Street itself.

La Guardia was not of course the first airfield to give the port of New York its new dimension. The first big one was at Newark, and was founded in the first flush of public excitement after Lindbergh's 1927 Atlantic flight (he had taken off in *The Spirit of St. Louis* from Roosevelt Field on Long Island, but came home on the cruiser *Memphis* via Sandy Hook). Four airlines operated out of Newark from the start, and by 1930 it was the busiest commercial airfield in the world, with direct flights to the West Coast (thirty-six hours) and record-breakers like Rickenbacker, Amelia Earhart, and Howard Hughes taxying in from everywhere. One day in the 1930s Mayor La Guardia arrived there on a commercial flight but refused to disembark. He had bought a ticket to New York, he said, not Newark. They flew him to a naval air base at Jamaica Bay, within his city limits, and he used the publicity to argue for a municipal airport of New York—La Guardia. New York was also the intended terminal of the German transatlantic airship services. The pioneer ships landed at Lakehurst in New Jersey, completing the west-bound flight from Germany in about sixty-five hours, and when they built the Empire State Building, in 1938, they topped it with an airship tower. I was shown an early plan for the development of Teterboro, now a field for private aircraft, which showed it littered all over with dirigibles, two to a hangar ("Neither snow nor rain," said the brochure, "storm or fair, shall stay the couriers of the air").

By way of Fokkers, DC-4s, Constellations, 707s, these early excitements gave birth to the John F. Kennedy Airport, née Idlewild, ironically situated at the edge of the Jamaica Bay Wildlife Refuge: probably the best-known, and arguably the most disagreeable airport on earth. Well over a thousand aircraft land and take off there every day, three or four hundred of them from abroad, shepherded down the airways by control systems of unbelievable complexity, stacked in high circling queues until the air space is cleared, and sweeping in to land majestically over the wastes of Jamaica Bay, where the duck no longer bother to shy at their passing, and the yachtsmen's ears are insulated against the noise by the sheer accretion of insensibility.

JFK, as everyone calls it, is about the size of Manhattan Island from 42nd Street to the Battery—5,000 acres of it, five miles long, mostly tidal marshland pumped dry. More than 30 international airlines use the airport, and 45,000 people work there. It was born in 1948, and ever since they have been building it. Architecturally it is a paean to the spirit of private enterprise. Let other, less fortunate metropoles impose a style upon their international airports, realizing the dead hand of public control. At Kennedy only the master plan would be imposed: for the rest, airlines could find their own solutions, building their own terminals to their own designs.

This has made the airport one of the most disturbing architectural complexes I know. It is like a world fair of uninhibited violence, unexampled flamboyance, and permanent prospects, and it is treated as a fair by millions of sightseers, who consider it a tourist spectacle outclassed in New York only by the Statue of Liberty and Rockefeller Center. It always looks to me as though with luck it may yet be dismantled, leaving only a Hall of Universal Understanding or a Tower of the Air, but it is really there to stay. There are many indeed who find its colossal clash of styles stimulating, and believe it properly to represent our century, and New York. It has certainly won, like most things in America, many awards. It is an Award-Winning Airport.

The general shape of the Kennedy terminal is a bulgy circle, with terminal buildings all around, passengers passing through their particular airline building to the waiting aircraft beyond. In the middle are shrines of various sorts, like the First National City Bank, the Police Control Building, and the Tri-Faith Chapel Plaza—a group of three humped structures, disconcertingly like tombs, in which the passenger may say a last prayer before stepping into his Mighty Aerial Giant and hurtling into the void. To the design of the circle itself, with all its variety of structures, some of the most celebrated architects of the century have contributed. It is an architectural museum of the fifties and sixties. Nobody appears to have consulted anybody else. Functional Brutalism glares haughtily across the Chapel Plaza at Contemporary Romantic, squares are snubbed by circles, horizontals by parabolas. The arrival buildings, which all airlines from overseas use, were designed by Skidmore, Owings and Merrill, and might be classified as Basic Unnoticeable. The Trans World Airlines building, on the other hand, is by Eero Saarinen, and seems to me one of the great sights of New York. It is all flying curves, all airy motion, with internal bridges, gently sweeping staircases, and carpeted alcoves— better suited temperamentally to balloons or gliders, perhaps, than to jets, but then again far more of the Jet Age than the Piston, and certainly superbly fitted to put the passenger into that mood of weightless unreality essential to the enjoyment of air travel. The American Airlines building, by Kahn and Jacobs, is decorated with an enormous multicolored mosaic which gives it a suggestively Mexican, or Inca, look. The Pan Am building, by Tippetts, Abbett, McCarthy, and

Stratton, is circular: aircraft actually nose their way into its shelter, and stand there all in a ring, rumps into the open air, like so many splendid cows at the milking machine. Eighteen foreign airlines share quarters adjacent to the arrival building, and they have contributed to the excitement by the wild variety of their décor, of which the silliest is undoubtedly that devised by KLM for the VIP lounge—in the middle of all this, within earshot of the jets, a chamber furnished throughout with seventeenth-century antiques.

I need hardly say that this vast complex of buildings, supplemented by freight terminals, offices, hangars, a large hotel, and every sort of ancillary structure, is already much too small for its functions, is being enlarged, modified, demolished, or rebuilt in all directions, and is fast catching up with that old Clipper terminal in its air of dated allure.

For by now the Giant Liners of the Sky throw themselves into New York at the rate of one every five minutes, and the entire function of the seaport, evolved through so many generations, has been reproduced in microcosm in the airports of the city. New York is now as much a port of the sky as of the sea: the elements are balanced.

Not long ago the President of the Borough of Queens, one of the five constituent boroughs of the city of New York, made the attractive if naïve suggestion that all night flying should be banned over the city: two of the three big airports are in his borough, and he wanted his constituents to get some sleep. Somebody gave me a copy of the reply he got from the Aviation Development Council, a body representing all branches of the aviation industry; and thumbing through this document idly one day, I realized how astonishingly intricate were the aerial activities of the city. I had often thought in the night hours of the pilots out at Sandy Hook, the Coast Guardmen at the Ambrose Light, the riding lights of the ships sailing through the Narrows, and all the other traditional nighttime images of the port. I knew very well, too, how many of the transatlantic flights took off at midnight. But it put the night, and the port, into a new perspective to learn that nearly 100 cargo aircraft left New York each night; that every night the New York fur industry made some 900 shipments by the night flights, while 3,000 pounds of fresh flowers were flown in from California, and several million pounds of strawberries, and 10,000 pounds of Chinese vegetables. The *New York Times* flies out each night to 10,000 American destinations, while 25,000 copies of the *Wall Street Journal* are flown *into* New York from its printers in Massachusetts. At night hundreds of thousands of servicemen are flown in and out of New York, and so much high finance is handled at the airports that if there were a night curfew, so the Council told the President of Queens, the New York banks would lose nearly $35 million a year in interest.

"I trust," concluded the signatory of this document, "this information will be helpful in understanding the situation." It was certainly helpful to me, for it is hard to grasp the staggering growth of air traffic in this city without a few homely illustrations. Ever since 1955 more passengers have been flying the Atlantic than have been going by sea; today the discrepancy is overwhelming—20 times as many. The vast majority of them fly from New York, as they always have. Air freight, too, has increased faster in New York than anywhere else in the world, and in value more cargo is airfreighted from this city than is sent out by sea from that old rival of the seaboard, Boston. Only two customs districts in the entire United States extract more revenue than does Kennedy Airport (and one of those two is the seaport of New York).

I was showered with statistics to prove these points, but

after a few days at the airports I did not have to be persuaded: so incessant is the flow of the traffic, so vastly automated are the new air-freight centers, and so powerful is the sense of inevitability to the process, as though it is organic to the city. At the moment it often expresses itself in appalling congestion, the aircraft queuing up in their scores upon the tarmac, the passengers miserably dragging out the waiting hours. Things must have felt rather the same in the heyday of South Street, when the New York packet ships were setting the pace of the seas, and the East River was jammed with sea traffic. Now, though, the atmosphere is not merely exciting, but actually alarming. How could they keep up, I wondered? Everywhere I went I heard of experiment: more aircraft, bigger aircraft, more cargo, more passengers week by week, more flights, the air bus, the supersonic transport, vertical take-off, helicopter taxis—"the exciting challenge," as I saw it described in a statement to the Senate Commerce Committee, "of the accelerating growth in the aviation industry." This was an understatement, I thought. It was like a whirlwind sweeping through the old port, blowing hats off, shaking buildings, ruffling the waters of the harbor, and sending every statistic, every last year's panegyric, helter-skelter to oblivion.

Chapter 7

LINERS

So now I conceived of the port in a double perspective, in height and in breadth, sea and sky. The tradition remained unbroken. JFK was recognizably a successor to South Street, the jets came from the same stud as *Sea Witch* and the *Flying Cloud*. Yet I could not help feeling that the true patricians of the port remained the Atlantic passenger liners. A mellow, slightly maudlin nostalgia surrounds their heyday, and attaches itself in a wan way even to the passenger liners of today, which are chiefly floating holiday camps, and make the Atlantic crossing more or less as a matter of form, between junketings to the Bahamas or interminable global cruises.

On a boat in the harbor once I met one of the last of the old-school New York shipping reporters, wearing a waxed mustache and a hat, and holding his hands authentically in his raincoat pockets, as in the old movies. Thirty years ago the men of his craft were near celebrities, so intimate was their acquaintance with *l'haute monde* of the Atlantic liners. They appeared at every shipboard party, addressed the great by their first names, and met all the incoming liners ceremonially at Sandy Hook. A friend of mine once told me that in childhood she called them the See-Off-Ship-Reporters, so allegorical a part did they play in the ritual of an Atlantic sailing.

My new acquaintance remembered those days with wry affection: ours is not a regretful trade. We stood together in the lee of the deckhouse that day, watching the harbor pass, and he told me tales of the waterfront when he was a cub reporter, and old jokes of the port. For half a lifetime he had come out on the Coast Guard cutter each day to meet the incoming liners, in the days when every film star sailing into New York on the *Aquitania* liked to distribute her views on life, marriage, and the state of Hollywood, and the diplomats of the world sped on the great steamships from crisis to negotiation. My friend had enjoyed himself. Everybody knew the ships then, he told me. Several morning newspapers carried columns of shipping news each day. "Why, it was news when a Prime Minister or an actress arrived in those days. All the photographers would be out here on the cutter, and the newsreel boys—we'd be sure of the front page every time. Nowadays nobody notices, they all travel so much. Liz Taylor's the only actress with news value. Nobody notices a politician at all, they fall in and out so often, in and out of that UN."

They are essences of the thirties that are distilled by the great liners, though the *idea* of scheduled sea services was born in this seaport more than a century earlier. In October 1817 it was announced in the New York papers that early in the following year a new kind of transatlantic service would begin. Four packet boats would maintain a regular monthly service between New York and Liverpool, leaving to schedule whether or not they were loaded to capacity, and having special accommodation for cabin passengers. The first to sail would be the *James Monroe*, 424 tons, Captain James Watkinson, which would leave from her South Street moorings on January 7th. Robert Albion, in his book *The Rise of New York Port,* calls this "a radical alteration in the habits of ships." Until then most ships had either been tramps or traders which sailed when the conditions were right—when the hold was full, when the winds were favorable. Half a dozen ships might sail for Liverpool in one week, and no more for a couple of months. Shipowners often announced "firm sailings," but everybody knew they were generally postponed when the time came; so the crowd that assembled to watch the departure of the *James Monroe,* Mr. Albion surmises, was probably fairly skeptical. All was ready, though. It was snowing heavily, but everything was snug and shipshape, the owners being anxious to make a good first impression. The seven passengers were on board. The cargo, mostly apples, was below decks. The bag of European mails had been rushed to the quay at the last moment. Captain Watkinson was by the wheel. Ten o'clock, came the chimes of St. Paul's Chapel through the snow; and as it rang, the first of the New York ocean liners, punctual to the dot, backed out of her berth and sailed away to sea.

A large black ball was the emblem of the service, and the Black Ball Line was the first of all the liner companies that have used the port of New York: proud dead lines of the past, like Inman or Collins, or lines long since absorbed in others' glories, like White Star, or the old perennials that are part of the sea's poetry—Holland-America, Cunard, French Lines, North German Lloyd, American President. As Mr. Albion says, since the sailing of the *James Monroe* "most of the crack liners of the world have made New York their western terminus."

The liners vastly increased the prosperity and importance of the port, shippers all along the Atlantic seaboard preferring to send their cargoes to New York to catch their reliable sailings. The ships progressed from sail to steam,

seven passengers to a couple of thousand, and became part of
the fabric of the city, and indeed of the nation—even in
1890 more than 15,000 Americans sailed into New York on
the liners each week, returning from pleasure or money-
making in Europe. Almost anybody of means had sailed on
the liners, stomaching in the early days not only harsh conditions, but often contemptuous captains too. "Here's a
story for your book," said my friend on the cutter. "There's
this Cunarder running through a thick fog on the Banks, and
here's this lady passenger up on deck breathing in the drama.
Along comes the captain. Oh captain, she says, is it always
foggy here like this? The captain strides by without a pause.
How the devil do I know, he says—*I don't live here!*"

By the turn of the twentieth century the comings and goings of the liners were part of the daily excitement of New
York, and the competition between the companies for the
mythical Blue Riband of the Atlantic was followed like a
ball game. The Black Ball packets averaged 22 days from
New York to Liverpool; by 1900 the steamers were doing it
in five, and year after year ships beating the west-bound
record would break a triumphal pennant from their topmast
as they passed the Ambrose Light. Terrific exertions were
made, too, to hasten the turn-round of liners: the Cunarder
Berengaria, for example, once docked in New York at 9 A.M.,
unloaded 1,000 passengers, 900 sacks of mail, and all her
freight, revictualed, refueled, reloaded, and sailed again at
midnight.

New Yorkers seem to have watched this competition with
sporting detachment. They were presumably pleased when
an American ship broke the speed record, but they appear to
have regarded all the great liners, whatever their nationality,
as more or less the property of the port. The great days of
the Atlantic Greyhounds are recalled with impartial affection. Murals in the older public buildings generally have one

somewhere in sight, usually in the act of passing the Statue of Liberty: the central hall of the Custom House has a splendid representation of a Hollywood Queen in full spate on the sun deck, the cameras whirling at her feet. Many New Yorkers remember the old liners in vivid detail, and love to recall the matchless dignity of the old *Ile de France,* or remind one gently that it was in fact the *Majestic,* not the *Berengaria,* which began life as the *Imperator.* Some ships are remembered very sentimentally: the *Mauretania,* a vessel everybody seems to have loved ("a Queen with a fighting heart," Franklin Roosevelt called her), or the *Leviathan,* for many years the largest ship to fly the American flag, which had been built in Germany as the *Vaterland* and was eventually returned there as bombs. The ritual welcome offered to new ships now is really a symptom of this nostalgia. The first appearance of a liner does not mean much to modern New York, but in the old days it was a properly civic event, like the opening of a new bridge, or the unveiling of a landmark. The comings and goings of that newcomer would be, for the next twenty years or so, part of the New York scene, and its silhouette, appearing for the first time so excitingly through the Narrows, would be universally familiar.

Several times I went out with the Coast Guard cutter to board an incoming liner, and sail with her up the Bay to Manhattan. Generally I found it a forlorn experience, so anachronistic do the great ships feel, and so much less exciting, to my tastes, than the punch and drumming of the jets. If the ship has been on a cruise, there is a cruel contrast between the atmosphere on the bridge, where the passage of the vessel is conducted with all the calm grandeur of tradition, and the scenes below, where the home-coming pleasure seekers cavort themselves in unsuitable textiles, and the only civilized corner of the dining saloon seems to be the alcove, discreetly tucked from public view, where the musicians, the comedians, and the chorus girls breakfast together with decorum.

If it is returning on the regular run from Europe, the ship is likely to be half empty, and there is pathos to the proceedings. With what determined jollity does the ship's band, middle-aged and loudly saxophonic, play the old favorites on the boat deck as the ship pulls in to the Manhattan pier! How forced are the smiles of the stewards, if they smile at all, dispiritedly surveying the prospect of gratuities as the soured divorcées and retired suburban realtors prepare to disembark! Gone are the diamonds, the repartee of actresses and literary lions, the jostling reporters, the duchesses instructing their maids or the statesmen urgently clutching their dispatch cases! I once came in to Pier 86 on the liner *United States*, the fastest ever built, and I watched the faces of the passengers around me, waiting for the gangplank to open as the band subsided into a last medley of patriotism—*America, America, Dixie, The Star-Spangled Banner,* and one or two stirring marches I did not recognize.

Trilly secretarial voices rang, as those grand old tunes reverberated, jeweled spectacles vibrated, and stiletto heels tapped the deck; but the expressions on the passengers' faces struck me as sad—as though the hum of the liner's mechanisms, the blaring of those anthems as the vessel docked, were taking the voyagers back for a moment to a lost American world, the world of Dorothy Parker, Robert Benchley, "Stars and Stripes Forever"—a world encapsulated there still between the decks of the great ship, that would dissipate the moment the gangplank doors were opened, and they returned to 46th Street.

Sometimes, nevertheless, I managed to recapture the magic of the liners for myself.

One way was to meet an Italian liner at the pier, direct

from Naples—the yachtlike *Cristoforo Colombo,* the strange *Raffaello* or *Michelangelo,* whose lattice smokestacks dominate the piers like helicopter platforms. The Italian ships still bring many immigrants to New York, and by hanging around down there, and watching from the walls, I used to experience vicariously some of the excitement of a liner's arrival, which has meant so much to New York down the generations. The passenger piers of Manhattan have long been a well-known disgrace, and though they are soon to be swept away and replaced with a dazzle of modernity, I shall remember them all my life as they are today. Their huge bare arrival sheds are icy cold in winter, impossibly stuffy in summer. Their colors are drab, their waiting rooms cramped, their porters surly, their floors dirty, their arrangements slipshod, their designs inept, their fittings derelict, their atmosphere unwelcoming and their architecture hideous. They accordingly stand foursquare in the tradition of American immigration, and the scene on Pier 90 when an Italian ship arrives is rich in piquant detail.

For hours before disembarkation the waiting rooms and windy platforms are crowded with the Italians of New York —only just casting off their black mantles and fustian suits, like moths emerging from chrysalides, to assume the brighter colors of Americans. The air smells of Italian cigarettes and garlic, like the Milan railway station when you first step off the train from Switzerland, and is full of Italian chatter and admonishment—Ricardo, Ricardo! Dove anda? Veni qua! Ricardo! *Ricardo!* Very old men with white mustaches gossip over hot dogs in corners. Ample dark-eyed girls hold hands silently with young men in pointed black shoes. All the Italian archetypes are here: the grandmothers in black, their legs cheerfully apart on the benches, the overdressed children, the handsome young Sicilians, the prickly old men with battered hats and the babies with pierced ears in canopied perambulators.

When the ship comes in most of this genial crowd, its patience only slightly worn, crowds into the forecourt outside the arrival hall, where one can see over the barriers to the customs desks inside. A youth is selling souvenirs at a stall—flags of Italy and the U. S. A., sailor caps with the ship's name on them. A man in a dark hat and a black coat has climbed onto a railing, and sits impassive above the crowd, gazing fixedly at the great white prow of the ship. A child in a red woolly helmet perches on somebody's shoulder, lethargically waving a balloon; upon the arm of an elderly woman all in black hangs a girl in bright pink slacks.

A few first-class passengers arrive first, carrying expensive suitcases, greeted by significant-looking men in heavy overcoats and walking hastily down the drafty platform to waiting limousines below. It is the tourist class the crowd awaits, and now it rustles with anticipation. There is a crackle on the loudspeakers. "They're coming now!" "Honest?" "Si, si, e vero, guarda, they come now!" But no, it is only a request for the representative of the Italian Welcome League, to report to the pier office. Sometimes the crowd swells through the movable barriers, and boorish security men chivvy it back—"*In*side, *in*side, move along lady, get back inside—hey you, d'you hear me, back behind the barriers!"

Now there is a real stir beyond the barriers; the policemen turn, and brace themselves; and out at last, into America, come the latest of all the packet-boat passengers. The first is a priest, strutting briskly through, wreathed in smiles, to be greeted by three colleagues like a trio of welcoming rooks. Then the rush begins. A young man suddenly escapes from the barrier and hurls himself like a projectile into the arms of his waiting relatives—his mother first, in an embrace like an orgy, then his father, then his three brothers more or less as a unity, then his mother again, then his three brothers separately, back to his father, and then in a wave of tears, cross-talk, hugs, and handshakings the whole family staggers, some of its members actually walking backwards, through the doors and out of sight. A splendid old lady in a velvet coat, harnessed with handbags, is greeted with deference by what I take to be her eldest daughter and her apprehensive son-in-law. A man in a wide gray hat, a white scarf in his overcoat, leans forward to pinch a young man's cheek, kneading it for a moment between finger and thumb before slapping him on the back and shepherding him breezily off-stage—as if to say that there's no time to be lost, there's money to be made, if he wants to make good like the rest of the family he'd better get down to the store and start work. It takes hours for the crowd to clear, and outside the pier building hundreds of people shiver despondently over their baggage, waiting for taxis; but in the end the last excited newcomer has disappeared into Manhattan, the ship is left to stock up with fuel and victuals, and only the tangy smell of foreign tobacco, the litter and the echo of emotions, remain to mark the arrival of another liner.

The other way I found to grasp the majesty of the Atlantic liners was to stand well away from them. From a distance they still look the embodiments of power, speed, and enterprise they once were. They look marvelous from the upper floors of office buildings, glorious incidentals to the New York scene as they slide downstream to the Bay. The distant sight of their smokestacks is good, too, high above the West Side terraces. Best of all, I used to enjoy standing on the sidelines of the harbor, on a Brooklyn pier or a Bayonne jetty, to watch the big ships gathering speed as, emancipated from their tugs, they paced towards the Narrows and the sea.

Once I saw the old *Queen Elizabeth,* the biggest of all the liners, pass by in this way. I was alone on the shore of Governors Island, in the shadow of an old fort the British built. It was a wonderfully clear autumn morning. The city seemed far away, the harbor looked empty, the only noises were the swish of the water, occasional cars, and shouts from the Coast Guard station behind me, and the airplanes above. Nowhere in the world can be more brilliant on such a day, the air more vibrant with life and chance, the sky more vast. It makes the spirit sing. In this frame of mind I was looking out across the upper bay, thinking elevated and affectionate thoughts, when suddenly around the corner of the fort appeared the *Queen Elizabeth*.

She looked out of scale at first, too big even for that setting, like a child's drawing of a ship beside a cardboard castle. She seemed to be utterly deserted, nobody apparently on her decks, no one to be seen on her bridge. She made no audible sound. But a thin vapor streamed from her funnels, the water foamed at her prow, and she appeared to be *flying* out to sea. I had never thought her a beautiful ship, but she looked ethereally beautiful that morning—eighty thousand tons of her leaping, unmanned, silent, exultantly through New York Bay. It was like prematurely seeing the ghost of a ship; or the ghost perhaps of all the great liners that have frequented this seaport, each prouder than the one before, all exultant in their day.

Chapter 8

THE GREETERS

Shortly before dawn at Battery Point, on a drizzly working day in winter: the early workers break with a rush from the Staten Island ferry, sprinting ashore like prisoners released, and the kind Italians in chefs' hats who run the coffee stall are doing a brisk business with coffee and donuts. A few layabouts are dozing in the shadows. A Negro woman, her hair done up in a chiffon scarf, bumps into a friend on the pavement. "Hey, lady," she cries, "where you been?" "Oh, around," says the other, "around, up and down"—and so they walk off together, talking fast but evasively, arm in arm into the dark.

At the Coast Guard building on the point, near the pier at which the Statue of Liberty ferryboat is still asleep at its moorings, a neat Coast Guard cutter is already wide awake. Lights burn in the wheelhouse, a sailor is doing something with ropes at the gangplank, now and then a car drives onto the pier, and a man muffled in a blue parka or a civilian overcoat hastens on board. "What d'ya want, the cutter?" asks the policeman at the gate. "Okay, that's the boat there, just ready to go, with the light there."

A bell, a shouted exchange, a roar of diesels, and she is

away into the fog. The bell buoys tinkle dismally in the fairway, and the downtown skyscrapers seem to be decapitated by the mist. Across the Bay the floodlighting of the Statue of Liberty is diffused across the low swirling cloud. New York lies in a damp hush. There goes the ferry again, ablaze with deck lights and moving fast, and there before the Narrows are the riding lights of the ships at the quarantine station. Under the great bridge now, as the swell from the sea makes the little ship roll, and the wind blows in fresher from the Atlantic; and presently there approaches out of the murk, as the first light of the day glimmers over Sandy Hook, the vastly towering form of a liner.

"There she is." The cutter pauses, turns, and is presently sailing in the lee of the ship, whose lights glimmer high above, and whose engines throb portentously. Closer and closer the little craft approaches, faster and faster the pace seems, until a small door opens in the flank of the liner, and a sailor's white face appears. He is like a man on a passing planet, peering out at the world. Soon there is only a gap of a foot or two between the big ship and the small, and one by one a group of men steps across from the Coast Guard cutter, helped by the seaman on the other side. First go the immigration and health people, then the customs men, one by one from the quivering cutter, then a man from the shipping company, and finally a couple of uniformed agents from Wells Fargo, carrying leather bags of money.

For so many years have the cutters been sailing out from Battery Point, to meet the big ships coming in, that the operation has acquired the casual assurance of a habit. New York is a very experienced port, and is always at work. Unaware though most citizens remain, night and day throughout their archipelago the cutters are sailing, the dredgers are dredging, the tower men are talking in the jets, the harbor pilots are going aboard, and the Wells Fargo men, swinging their treasure bags with panache, are stepping across that gap.

Of all the institutions I came across in New York, the one I liked best was the Benevolent Association of Sandy Hook Pilots. It has a guild or fraternity flavor to it unusual in this city, and is salty, and evidently efficient, and agreeably pleased with itself.

There have been professional pilots in this harbor since the port began. Until the 1830s they were appointed by the State Governor, and there was an official monopoly of pilotage. When it was abandoned, cutthroat competition followed. New York and New Jersey pilots fought each other for custom, the speedy little pilot cutters raced each other to meet incoming ships or sailed further and further out to sea—sometimes two hundred miles from harbor. The pilots were superlative seamen, in a city of seamanship. Pilot boats were often chartered to undertake quick missions overseas. One of them crossed the Atlantic in 1812 to warn American captains in Europe that war had broken out with England; she was chartered by the merchants of New York, and took her news as far as Gothenburg and Archangel before scudding home to the Bay. In the war itself the pilots became disgracefully successful privateers, preying on the innocent British shipping making for Halifax. The original yacht *America* was a New York pilot schooner, and her captain in the famous 1851 race was a Sandy Hook pilot.

Later in the century the New York pilots began to accumulate dignity, and they presently became, almost to a man, people of stately presence. They habitually boarded their ships wearing frock coat, silk hat, and gloves, and in 1887, I learn from Charles Edward Russell's book *From Sandy Hook to 42°*, they were "evidently of the sea and yet not of it, notably well-dressed, notable not less for a certain look of intelligence and command, the unmistakeable look of the executive." The description is wonderfully borne out by a photograph I was once shown of Captain Electus Comfort, forty-two years a New York pilot, around the end of the century. He is a very grand Victorian gentleman, wearing his silk hat and his frock coat, also a waistcoat, a bow tie, a big gold watch chain, and superb white whiskers. He leans elegantly upon a chair back, standing, with his legs crossed at the ankle, smoking a cigar; and he gazes patriarchally over the photographer's left shoulder, with a trace of condescension—not unlike the manner I fancied in the towers of Manhattan, as they surveyed the commotion of the harbor a few chapters back.

Much of this old splendor, and all the expertise, has been inherited by the Benevolent Association, which now includes all the harbor pilots. It likes to trace direct descent from the original New York pilots of 1694, and claims frankly enough to be the finest pilotage service in the world—which it probably is. One of my favorite statistics concerns the "rate of incidents" recorded during the pilotage of ships into this port in the years 1962 to 1967. During that time the Sandy Hook pilots brought in rather more than 123,000 ships. The rate of incidents was $8\%_{1000}$ of 1 per cent—of which 88 per cent, the pilots add defensively, "were of a minor nature."

Permanently drifting near the Ambrose Light is the pilot cutter *New York* or its deputy the *New Jersey*. These comfortable vessels form the pilots' floating base. When a ship comes in from sea, a pilot boards it from the *New York* to take it into the harbor; when a ship comes out of the Bay, its pilot is dropped to await an incoming charge. Pilots are always available, every hour of the year, and they must sometimes clamber aboard incoming ships in very uncomfortable circumstances—"Note," as one of their publications wistfully remarks: "A good sturdy and clean ladder is always appreciated by your pilots."

Sometimes they fall in, and this must be a distressing sight, for they are still a stately body of men. I shall never forget the pilot who brought in the Dutch liner *Rotterdam*, one day when I was coming into New York upon her bridge. The master of the ship was impressive enough, all crags and eyebrows, but the pilot was superb. He looked like the president of a bank, in his brown hat and business suit, and his calm was lordly. He only made one request of the captain, as he guided the ship smoothly through the upper bay. Might he have, he asked most courteously, for his collection, a picture postcard of the vessel? I once had lunch with four Sandy Hook pilots at a lavish downtown club, and though the occasion was merry, still I was conscious always that I was being entertained by men of stature. "Sure thing, cap'n, yessir," the waiters deferentially said, when another round was ordered, and when we stepped into the elevator it seemed to me that the crowd of business people made way carefully for those four stalwart men of the sea, as though the safety of the descent depended upon them.

It takes fifteen years to qualify as a pilot, just about as long as it took Gibbon to write *The Decline and Fall of the Roman Empire*. Boys usually apply at fourteen, and usually join at twenty-two, after college or military service. They spend the first eight years as odds-bodies on the pilot boats. If all goes well, they are then registered as apprentices, and get Deputy Pilot's Licenses. Then for the next seven years they learn the handling of ships in the harbor, undergoing examinations every year, until at last, as they approach middle age, they are recognized as first-class pilots, licensed to handle any ships afloat in the approaches to New York. This must be the longest of all indentures, and many young men drop out, disillusioned by the deck swabbing, or envious of less exacting curricula ashore. The compensations are great, though. The money is very good in the end. The pilots are their own masters, governed only by their own co-operative association. The job is satisfying, and a Sandy Hook pilot need not retire until he is seventy—though in his last five years, ocean passengers may be relieved to hear, he is disqualified from handling the very largest liners.

There are 142 pilots, and they are normally on a two-hour standby. When the telephone rings, night or day, they must leave their comfortable suburbs and drive at once to the docks; and before three hours are gone, while Valley Stream or Hoboken has made its beds, totted up a page of its accounts, or exhausted the subject of Wendy's infatuation for that impossible young man from the real-estate office, your Sandy Hook pilot is on the bridge of his ship, munching a sandwich, politely murmuring his instructions to the helmsman, and keeping his eyes steady on the Richmond Channel.

And at that same moment, too, in the half-light of the control towers at Kennedy, Newark, and La Guardia, the air controllers are guiding *their* craft through other channels of the port. Here is a very different scene. In its tense and urgent concentration, its flickering lights and clutter, it reminds me of a television studio, transmitting live. The air controllers are insulated against the world outside, clamped in their high towers far more remotely than on any liner's bridge, and often caged in there with steel doors for security. The pressure is terrible. From the flicks and dots of the radar screens one may get some impression of the weaving patterns of aircraft invisible above one's head—approaching or leaving the three great airports, stacked up over Long Island, overflying to Chicago or Montreal—airliners from Europe, military aircraft from Floyd Bennett Field on Long

Island, private aircraft by the hundred, Coast Guard seaplanes—flights from a couple of hundred cities of the interior, helicopters, troop transports—all in motion somewhere out of sight, or lined up at Kennedy waiting to leave, or suddenly streaking into view outside the tower window—*"Look at that fool! Keep moving, you bastard, keep moving!"*

Here nobody aspires to dignity. The controllers are mostly thin young men in shirt sleeves, looking very tired. Some are talking into their microphones, some are glued to radar screens, some are taking a few minutes off. None are at rest. They fidget all the time, moving here and there, trailing the wires of their headsets, leaning forward to look into the sky. They are like prisoners who have been given shots of adrenalin, to keep them on their feet.

In this restless dedication, which has an avant-garde suggestion to it, as though they are young artists up there devising concrete poetry—in this nerve-racked vigil they are properly adapted to the traffic they control, distinctly highly strung itself. The airports, though, are only a young part of an old harbor, and when the jets have landed at Kennedy another kind of functionary waits to welcome them. He is the airport's Greeter, a very courtly man, who offers a formal welcome to all royalty, all returning American Ambassadors, and the more distinguished foreign statesmen. I asked him what he said to them. "Well, I go out there and I say Welcome to the United States, on behalf of the Port of New York Authority." This seemed to me a medieval kind of function, akin to town-crying or calling the night hours; and I relished the picaresque contrast he offered, so suave, genial, and confident, to those cloistered young technicians in the tower above, bringing the aircraft down to earth.

Among the elms of Governors Island live the men of the Coast Guard service, with their boats, their wives, and their staunch traditions. They are always awake, too, and have been familiar in these parts since the American Revolution, for they are directly descended from the Revenue Cutter Service established with the Republic. There is an Admiral on Governors Island, whose command extends from Florida to New England, and includes four of the weather ships on station far out in the Atlantic. The Port Captain of New York is a Coast Guard officer, and the service has five ocean cutters based on the island, innumerable suave patrol boats, and five tugs which double as icebreakers. The Coast Guard are the traffic policemen of the harbor. They tend the buoys, man the lighthouses, run the lifeboats, convey officialdom here and there, and make themselves generally indispensable.

I spent several mornings on Governors Island, trying to see the port through their eyes. It looks fearfully confused from there, and the reports and orders flow in like memos to a casualty ward. There is a fire on a quay at Staten Island. Oil pollution off the Con Ed plant at 75th Street. A crane barge is sunk in the Arthur Kill. A diabetic seaman needs immediate hospital treatment from the steamship *Transunion*. There's a restriction on teletype and radio traffic because of a naval exercise. A load of confiscated weapons is to be ditched off the Ambrose Light. A man has jumped off the Staten Island ferry. Provide harbor welcome for motorship *Birkenfels*. A seaman on a tanker at Stapleton Anchorage is "acting in a highly irrational manner no indication alcohol." Provide harbor tour for visiting Interpol group. Body of a fifteen-year-old-girl found in water off College Point. Swash Channel lighted gong buoy is missing from its station—warn mariners.

The Coast Guard took it laconically, I thought, as though they were used to worse. Most of their officers have served in rougher waters and crueler climates than these. Some have worked on the Atlantic weather ships, many more have done

Arctic duty. In winter, resuming their astrakhan hats, they take their icebreakers up the Hudson to keep the passage open to Albany. The spectacle they offer then, shoving their way between the high wooded banks of the river, is astonishingly northern, and brings home how close this southern harbor lies to the inland immensities of Canada. Another reminder of wider horizons is an institution the Coast Guard runs called AMVER—Automated Merchant Vessel Report. This is an international system of ship tracking, designed to enable merchant vessels to help each other in trouble. Every day several hundred ships report to New York their positions and courses. These facts, together with various pertinent notes about the ships themselves—whether they have search radar, whether they carry doctors, their radio schedules —are fed into a computer: if any ship reports an emergency, anywhere in the world, the press of a button tells the Coast Guard what other merchant ships are near, and how qualified they are to help.

All this gives a kind of private excitement to Governors Island: the presence of all those distant ships, bottled so to speak in the AMVER computer; the constant ticking, whirring, and disgorging of the machine; the fleet of launches bobbing at their piers; and all that flow of information, that ceaseless bulletin of mishaps and obligations, which is like the register of an intelligence agency, its eye on every corner of the port.

An eavesdropper with a radio receiver can hear a peculiar sound, if he listens during the docking of a ship in New York. It is a kind of slurred stylized monologue, rather like the cadences of tobacco auctioneers. The voice is pitched on a flat and mournful plane, and varies not a semi-tone. "In Dorothy," it intones, "out Lucy. Dorothy port a quarter. Joan ahead easy." It is how one imagines a surgeon might talk, as he calls for his scalpel: it is in fact a tugmaster, directing the work of his team of vessels from the bridge of the liner they are docking.

The Coast Guard, the air controllers, the Sandy Hook pilots do their work out of the public sight, so that New Yorkers take them unremarked for granted. Not so the tugs. Tugs are essential to the Manhattan scene. They figure in every ceremonial occasion of the harbor, hooting among the fire-floats at maiden arrivals, or modestly in the background of regattas. Every sort of tug frequents this bay. There are ocean tugs, river tugs, tugs for towing barges, tugs for docking ships, tugs that look like ponies, tugs that look like ducks, red tugs, black tugs, dirty tugs, spotless tugs, and two high-funneled railway tugs, now to be seen taking it easy in their Hudson River moorings, which are the last steam tugs to work within the harbor of New York.

Tugs do not come cheaply in New York. Large liners generally need the help of three to swing them in to the North River piers (the old *Queen Elizabeth* took six), and the job is likely to cost the shipowner anything up to $3,000, depending on the time of day—far more at weekends, which is one reason why so few ships berth in New York on Sundays. The towboats have prospered in New York since the birth of steam, when ferryboat captains would sometimes peel away from their scheduled routes, to the consternation of their passengers, to earn a fast buck pulling in a sailing ship.

The best known of the New York tug companies is the Moran Towing and Transportation Co., Inc. I spent many hours with the Moran people, from Admiral Moran the chairman, a wiry reserve admiral with a taste for marine paintings and a distinguished war record, to the cook of the *Dorothy Moran*, a German who spent most of the Second World War marooned with his ship at Yokohama, and thought them the best years of his life. The tug control room is high in an office block above the Battery, a quiet sunny place with a marvelous harbor view, where men in white shirts talk gently into telephones disposing the movements of the tugs below— a different world, moving to a very different pace, from the control rooms of the airports. They can see far down the harbor to the Verrazano bridge, and well up the North River too; and there was scarcely a moment, during my own visits to the place, when none of their tugs were in sight.

Life on the tugs themselves seemed to me very agreeable, in fine weather at least: long hours of leisurely waiting about, punctuated by periods of intense activity. The boats are mostly equipped for deep-sea jobs, with bunks and a generous galley, and the food is excellent. I remember with a fairly languid pleasure a morning spent on one such boat. Some of the time we were tied up on the North River, feeding a friendly dog on the quayside, watching the ships go by, talking harbor lore and drinking coffee. Part of the time we were docking the liner *Raffaello*, with two sister tugs in company, and then for an hour or so the whole boat seemed to quiver with skilled concentration—the engineer with his reverberating diesels below, the skipper in shirt sleeves, sunglasses, and a plastic peaked cap on the back of his head, preoccupied but still polite at the helm. Down from the white mountain of a ship above came that monkish voice— "Joan ahead easy," "Kathleen ahead easy," "Easy off," "Hard away"—and each enigmatic command was answered with the bleep of a whistle, like a litany response.

The ship safely docked, off we went downstream again to lie in the sunshine until the next assignment; and so the long day passed in fits, starts, and gossip. A great sense of confidence attended the little craft. It all seemed so easy. The New York towboat crews are real harbor men, familiar with every creek and shallow, riding the currents of the Bay not always gracefully, indeed, for the modern tug is a burly mechanism, but with a commanding expertise.

They are the last of the greeters. Welcome to the port of New York, they seem to say, presenting their account and casting off: and so the cargoes, air or sea, human or inanimate —even dead or alive, for corpses in coffins regularly arrive at Kennedy Airport—are dumped upon the seaport's quays.

Chapter 9

THE PROCESSORS

Over the years New York has evolved an elaborate system of acceptance—the techniques by which all these arriving substances are examined, checked, and shoved away up the quayside, to be absorbed into the grinding mechanism that is the city itself. I use mechanical metaphors because the more I pottered around the immigration sheds, the custom houses, the quarantine piers, the more I felt that by now, after so many generations of practice, the processing was virtually automatic. It reminded me of some gigantic old plant, steam-operated I think, wheels, cogs, and pulleys always moving, into which sacks of miscellaneous matter are poured night and day to be mashed, sorted, and spewed out again. I could almost hear the hum of the gears—sometimes the squeaks too.

Just inside the Narrows is the quarantine station. Most ships stop there for clearance by the health authorities, and are to be seen lying off-shore with a look of morose resignation, like patients in the waiting room. Ships carrying doctors need not stop. The inspectors are interested chiefly in infectious disease, of course, but they are also looking for rats, those cosmopolitan villains, whose resident fleas, ticks, and miscellaneous microbes are very undesirable immigrants.

In the past rat-borne cholera was a constant danger. In 1892 two ships arrived with cholera on board, and all other ships from Europe were delayed indefinitely at quarantine. Among them was the liner *Normannia,* which had no cholera aboard, and whose passengers unfortunately included J. P. Morgan and other New York bigwigs. The health authorities nervously allowed her to proceed, but when she came to dock angry New Yorkers forcibly prevented her passengers from disembarking. Morgan at once bought another ship, transferred to her, and was landed elsewhere. The other passengers, having less ready cash to hand, were stranded on the *Normannia* day after day, getting understandably angrier themselves, until at last the shamefaced authorities actually bought the western end of Fire Island, off Long Island, including a secluded summer hotel, and dumped the whole lot there. They were eventually taken to their homes under the protection of the National Guard and the Navy.

Even more feared than cholera, throughout the history of the port, has been the bubonic plague—Europe's Black Death. Its bacteria can infect any sort of rat, or the fleas that live upon rats, and in fact it is endemic to the United States, as it is to most countries. Since 1925, though, there has not been a bubonic epidemic among American humans, and this is because infected rats have never been able to get a foothold in infected areas. In New York it would not take many specimens of *Pasteurella pestis* to set off a plague. There is alleged to be a rat for every human in the port, of three separate but equally repulsive genera, and they appear to be surviving the worst that exterminators, cats, and rat-proof architecture can do (the worst of all, I am convincingly told, is poisoned peanut butter): in 1969 a colony of several hundred, migrating from Harlem, boldly implanted themselves upon the center strip of Park Avenue at its poshest point, between 58th and 59th Streets, constructing a labyrinth of burrows beneath the street, and astonishing Sunday morning pedestrians by assembling *en masse* to gorge themselves upon the pigeons' leftovers. The plague germ would spread irresistibly among this underground army of rodents, skulking in every sewer and every wharf, frequenting the garbage cans in the small hours, and weighing anything up to a pound and a half. Some people say the New York rats are the biggest in the world: they have been known to swim the Hudson River, and they are fearfully astute.

When a ship puts in, then, one of the first tasks of the public-health officials is to look for rats on board. Sniff, sniff, prod, prod go the inspectors through the bowels of the ship, smelling for the peculiar pungent odor of the rat, for droppings or nests or tracks. Ships often have rats aboard. If there are not too many, tear gas bombs are thrown about the vessel, to flush out any human stowaways, and then a more lethal gas is released. The dead animals are sent to the public-health station on Staten Island, where ghastly serums are made of their organs and parasites, and injected into guinea pigs to see if they contain the bubonic germ.

This has been routine for nearly half a century. Generations of guinea pigs have suffered for the safety of New York, and never once has the plague been shipped into the city. In January 1943, however, the French freighter *Wyoming* arrived out of the Atlantic in a convoy from Casablanca, and its captain produced a certificate declaring that the ship had already been fumigated. The overworked authorities took his word for it and allowed the ship to dock. A day or two later longshoremen working on her reported that there were rats on board, so she was fumigated again. Twenty rats were gassed. On Staten Island they brewed the usual serum, inoculated a standard guinea pig, and a few days later were horrified to discover that they had isolated *Pasteurella pestis:* the guinea pig was dead.

It was wartime, the port was tense, and the authorities slapped a cover of absolute secrecy upon what they called "the *Wyoming* matter." Nobody knew how many rats had already got ashore. The ship had moved from berth to berth in New York, had tied up in Brooklyn, Manhattan, and Staten Island, and might have discharged infected rodents at all three. Teams of exterminators went urgently into action, laying traps around the three piers, and assiduously avoiding waterfront reporters. For five months every rat they caught was sent for autopsy. None were infected. By the end of May it was concluded that by a merciful stroke of fortune none of the plague rats had disembarked from the *Wyoming;* but it was not until Joseph Mitchell told the story in the *New Yorker,* a year later, that the people of the seaport knew how close they had been to the Black Death of the ancients.

Fumigated, inoculated, or smoked out with tear gas, New York's human cargoes are passed on to that old archetype of this Bay, the immigration officer. For generations this dark distant figure cast a blot upon the American reputation, from the sad scenes of Ellis Island to those squalid appointments at the United States Consulate, only a few years ago, at which one was fingerprinted for one's three-week visit to the promised land. American immigration arrangements have been vastly improved in the past decade; but this is still not a branch of the United States Public Service for which the world at large yet feels any inexpungeable affection.

New York has traditionally been its home ground. Nowadays more immigrants enter the United States across the southern frontier from Mexico, but the whole ethos of immigration is still best summed up in this Eastern seaport. George Washington's original scheme of immigration was gloriously generous: "The bosom of America is open to receive not only the opulent and respectable stranger, but the oppressed and persecuted of all nations and religions." The original immigration laws were concerned only to keep out undesirables: prostitutes, oriental slave labor, epileptics, anarchists, beggars, people with "loathsome diseases," people whose passages were paid by others, illiterates, persons of constitutional inferiority, alcoholics, vagrants, stowaways, subversives. There were no such things as visas throughout the nineteenth century. Immigrants merely booked their passages, often extremely uncomfortable and shamefully expensive, and hoped for the best: if they were admitted, well and good, if not back they went again.

It was in the 1920s that the quota system was devised. This was intended to freeze the ethnic balance of the nation—which was the social and political balance, too—and for the first time to control the *number* of immigrants. Aryan peoples were allotted large quotas, Latins smaller ones, Slavs smaller still, Asians and Africans virtually no quota at all. This satisfied racial assessments current then all over the world, and by no means universally discredited now. It doubtless seemed perfectly just to most New Yorkers—the elite of the port was Anglo-Saxon, Dutch, or Anglophile Jewish, and the prosperity of the harbor was founded upon old associations with Nords. The night before the system came into force, on August 1, 1921, a fleet of 20 immigrant ships, with 25,000 passengers, assembled in the lower bay, outside the Narrows; and at midnight all these ships raced desperately into the harbor, in a rush to ensure their passengers places on their national quotas. It was one of the most extraordinary scenes in New York history, the steamers belching black smoke as they churned their way through the Narrows, the anxious passengers, like aspirants at some unrepeatable bargain sale, crowded on deck waiting to leap into the barges for Ellis Island.

These were the great days of the immigration lawyers, as they twisted or circumvented the Act to obviate a clause or find a special category. The New York papers of the 1920s carry many curious items of immigration news. Balkan aristocrats appeal against expulsion; Lithuanian Jews are admitted after rabbis intervene; gentlemanly Britons, I regret to report, are not infrequently unmasked. Often people tried to evade the quota restrictions by declaring themselves to be artistic performers, and therefore eligible for special entry. In 1924, for example, Miss Regina Kohn proved her claim with "a rendition of *Träumerai* upon the violin"; while "K. Becker, German midget," who was detained because the German quota was exhausted, announced to the Press that he would "play the cornet to the authorities next morning."

All this ended when visas were introduced, and immigrants were vetted before they left their own countries, but it was not until 1967 that President Johnson, in a ceremony at the Statue of Liberty, formally decreed the abolition of the quota system: immigrants could once more come to the United States irrespective of race, provided they had the skills or abilities the nation needed. Many of today's immigrants, especially those from Germany and Britain, are highly qualified professional people, who arrive in unobtrusive comfort carrying lucrative contracts, and would almost invariably have been disqualified in Washington's day for having their passage "paid by others." But many simple people still arrive in the old way, off crowded ships at the Manhattan piers as we saw that cold morning a few pages back—no longer packed off to Ellis Island, but still recognizable descendants of the immigrants in the old pictures, those gaunt weary men and kerchiefed women who seem to bear the weight of the ages on their backs.

The Department of Immigration is sensitive to those chill pierhead scenes, and aware of its own unhappy image. Its officials would prefer their work to be represented by the system at JFK, and they invited me to spend an evening in one of the booths there. This was an unexpectedly moving experience. The transatlantic aircraft arrive in waves: in the afternoon only a handful land at Kennedy, in the evening they all come in a rush, those from Rome, London, Paris, or Frankfurt, their passengers pressing on each other's heels into the immigration hall, and queueing resignedly, cluttered with passports and airline bags, for the officials in the booths. This is immigration in the contemporary style. Svelte Civil Service girls in blue uniforms totter tightly here and there, welcoming people, and the officially encouraged manner of the immigration officers is one of avuncular propriety: they generally know enough of most major languages not only to ask for an American address or a maternal grandparent's nationality, but even to offer an elementary pleasantry.

I stood in the background of the booth as the passengers came through, looking I suppose like some unusually well-disguised secret service agent, and it was revealing to see what emotions passed through their eyes, when they noticed me there: suspicion nearly always, ingratiation very often, sometimes a hint of collusion, and occasionally a look I had never encountered before, which I took to be fear. The officers treated every arrival, so far as I could see, precisely the same: a brisk look at the papers, a practiced reference to the black book, an almost automatic reflex of badinage, with those passengers who nervously offered a remark: "Oh, please don't look at my picture there, I look *terrible*"—"It's like we always say, ma'am, if you look as sick as you do in your passport, you're not fit to travel." Then the passport is stamped, the bits and pieces are collected, the inspector says

The oldest bridge: Brooklyn

Tugs, Hudson River

New York harbor pilot

At the Fulton Street fish market

The newest bridge: Verrazano

next please, welcome to the United States, and another immigrant goes on her way rejoicing.

It is considerately done now, and compares well in my experience with the formulas of other countries—except perhaps those agreeably undeveloped nations, all muddle and high spirits, at whose immigration desks one feels there is really no formula at all, only a cheerful approximation of ritual. Even so there is still poignancy to the scene at JFK. Some of the passengers that evening had clearly roistered their way across the Atlantic with champagne and canapés. Others, especially the mothers, the squirmy children, the stout beldames with swollen feet, arrived exhausted in that frenzied airport, into the glaring lights, the unremitting noise and movement of the New World; and as they looked wearily from the inspector to me, searching I imagine for some warmth of understanding in our faces, I sometimes thought I detected a flicker of regret in theirs.

A whiz of the mechanism, a whir, a sharp shove in the small of the back, and the incoming commodity is face to face with the customs men. The first thing they look for is agricultural produce, in case you are introducing pests to the United States. "You from Wales?" they said to me once. "Keep any stock there? *Donkeys?* Okay, follow me please"— and trundling my bags between us, we entered a Disinfectant and Disposal Room, where they sponged my shoes with liquid from a bucket, to remove any last fragments of foot-and-mouth disease. A kind of vat was bubbling in there, and into it men in white laboratory coats were tipping bagfuls of exquisite tropical fruits, mangoes and papayas and stems of bananas, enriching the hygienic air with lush and steamy smells. "What a waste," I said. "Sure is," they dispassionately replied, shoveling in a clutch of avocados and a pomegranate.

The Customs Service, like the Department of Immigration, works to long-established standards, sticks to its rules, and tries not to let a Venezuelan melon past its scrutiny. There have, as we British know too well, always been customs and revenue men in the American seaports, taxing tea or assessing whiskies. Their headquarters in New York stands appropriately upon the site of the original Fort Amsterdam, as if to remind the citizenry that upon the profits of portage this city has been built. The building is imposing. It overlooks Bowling Green, at the foot of Broadway, in that marvelously jumbled corner of lower Manhattan which links the waterfront with the financial district, and it is decorated with allegorical sculptures of continents and seaports, ranged with crests and symbols along the pediment. A dauntingly dignified staircase gives access to the halls above; and there embedded in huge *fin-de-siècle* offices, their great windows looking out towards sea and Stock Exchange, the Customs Service unremittingly broods.

I say broods because its officials often gave me, in conversation, an impression of remorse: not remorse indeed at catching smugglers, Heaven forbid, but remorse at having possibly let some through. Much the most interesting part of their work is not, of course, the everyday examination of suitcases at pier and airport, but the intricate and often protracted detective work behind the scenes. Prohibition offered them their most exciting times of all: with the Coast Guard, for years they were engaged in a running battle with the bootleggers smuggling liquor into New York—the greatest market for hard drink in the United States, and a city it is almost impossible to conceive as compulsorily teetotal. It was a sea battle. At first ships loaded with liquor anchored outside the three-mile limit off Sandy Hook, and were met there at night by fast launches. This regular assembly of ships was known as Rum Row, and the smugglers relied upon the speed of their launches to evade the revenue men. The Federal Government next announced that in this context territorial waters would be considered to extend twelve miles from the coast, and the battle then became a more subtle contest of intelligences. Now not only the revenue cutters tried to intercept the liquor launches, but speedboats of hijackers too, until at night the whole New York seaboard seethed with cops and robbers. Sometimes the bootleggers sailed their cargoes imperturbably into the harbor itself, even occasionally to the Manhattan piers. More often they went ashore on empty Long Island beaches, or on the New Jersey coast. One of the most successful gangs operated a fleet of six steamships and twenty fast launches, controlled by radio from a mansion overlooking Sandy Hook whose lower walls were steel-plated and whose approaches were guarded by machine guns.

I suppose drug smuggling is the contemporary equivalent of bootlegging. The New York customs are sharp with drugs. They are also concerned with illegalities as varied as "dumping" (selling foreign goods at prices unfair to American competition) and trading with China. The service has its own independent investigation agency in New York, empowered if necessary to investigate the Customs Commissioners themselves: its agents even go so far, they told me, as to look through the gossip columns of neighborhood newspapers, on the off chance that Mrs. van Fink has been showing off a dress she bought during her recent trip to Europe, but forgot to declare.

New Yorkers are always grumbling about their customs men, and the excesses of diligence they show at the airport, but they always seem to me less awful than the ones we have at home; and at least one must grant the Commissioners of Custom, down at Bowling Green in their palace of symbolisms, that they have made the port of New York, air and sea, far and away the most profitable customs region in the United States: the place where Mrs. van Fink, like the speedboat bootleggers of old, is least likely to get away with it.

Five hundred cranes, my pamphlets said, and 5,000 lighters disembarked the sea freight at 200 slips along New York's 750 miles of waterfront. There are still many places in the Bay where I could watch it handled the old way, in one of those vignettes of port life that marine artists of the twenties used to love. The black rusted hulk of the ship rises monumental above the quay, the sweating longshoremen labor deep in the hot hold, the bales and bags and boxes, the cars or banana bags, bits of machinery or knobbly packages are piled colorfully upon the wharf. The noise is terrific. Fork trucks scurry about. The dockers seem to shout a lot. Huge trucks are jammed hugger-mugger into the side streets behind the pier, wedged all crookedly beneath the elevated highway, or edging with racing engines and foul exhausts into the loading bays. It is the traditional daily performance of the universal dockside drama. It has undertones of waterside violence and commercial romance. Everywhere in this seaport, Perth Amboy to Long Island City, it is still enacted every day of the year, as it has been with minor variations of manner since the steamships first arrived.

Here and there in the archipelago, however, one may see the signs of a revolution: one of those infrequent moments in transport history, like the advent of steam or the invention of the screw propeller, when all the attitudes of the industry shift, and half the old ideas are discredited. In this revolution New York has played a leading part, as it did in all the others.

Air freight is part of it. The air-freight centers at Kennedy and Newark Airports are the two busiest in the world: New

York has seized upon this new method of portage with all the gusto that gave it pre-eminence in the Atlantic sea trade. There is not much to say about the process, which is (the aircraft apart) much less picturesque than those old dockside scenes. There are no precedents to shatter, no customs to adapt, and as one watches the impeccable crates flow smoothly through the automated freight sheds of the airports, data-processed, computer-fed, one can only stand back and marvel. The rate of growth is phenomenal. The tonnage of air cargo passing through New York increased five times between 1960 and 1966, and by 1967 the port's air cargo was worth a quarter of all New York's foreign trade (for if anyone wants to ship diamonds or rubies nowadays, they ship them by air). By 1968, as we and the President of Queens discovered, every kind of commodity was air-freighted in and out of New York—foodstuffs out of season, furs in a hurry, orchids from the tropics, monkeys for Welfare Island. Manufacturers who used to have distribution centers in other parts of the country do without them now, for they can deliver goods in the same time direct from New York. A Dutch piano maker has altered the shape of his instruments destined for New York, to pack them easier in aircraft holds. The saddest flights into JFK, during my stay in New York, were those that brought home the war dead from Vietnam.

The container is the second instrument of the portage revolution. At Port Elizabeth, on Newark Bay, I was taken one sunny winter morning to see a container ship unloaded. This was something new to me. For the most part cargo has been put on board ships in the same way at least since the days of the clippers: that is to say, crated according to the size and shape of the commodity, and stacked where there was space in the hold or on deck. This is the process that has given the waterfront its familiar cluttered or bumpy look. The quay at Port Elizabeth hardly looked like a quay at all. It was an enormous expanse of open yard, several hundred acres of it, in which the silvery steel container boxes were meticulously arranged as if for an orderly-room inspection. Each had been filled with its goods far away in the factory, and sealed for shipment; now they had merely to be slotted into place in their specially built ship. All was order on the quay. The trailer-trucks, far from jostling and grumbling their way towards the wharf, raced about as they pleased, with all the room in the world; and the whole place seemed preternaturally clean, as though it had been scoured by ascetic winds of change.

As for the ship awaiting its cargo at the quay, it looked less like a freighter than a whale factory. Almost gone, I realized that morning, were the last aesthetic links between the ocean cargo ship and the old sailing vessels. The great bulk carriers, oil or ore, long ago weakened the pedigree. Now the last rake of the prow is lost, the last graceful cut of the stern, the last touch of embellishment, figurehead or stern device, added to a freighter just for beauty's sake. This was pure machine. As a tank is no more than a gun with a vehicle to carry it, so a container ship is no more than a floating crate. So quick is the turn-round, fast enough to abash the officers of the *Berengaria* herself, that often members of the crew, having sailed halfway round the world with their cargo, do not bother to go into Manhattan.

All this gave me a queer feeling: all seemed so detached, so clinical, so insulated. Everywhere in the harbor I now observed the telltale gleam of the containers, piled on wharfs, loaded on the decks of ordinary ships, or slid like silver coffins into the maws of these queer new vessels. Around the expressways the container trucks speed to and from the port, and up the railway tracks beside the Hudson River the container trains travel with a certain eerie reticence—for who knows what those trim sealed receptacles have inside

them, clinking their way so blandly over the tracks? At Port
Elizabeth that day I was invited to lunch with a director
of one of the container-ship companies, in their beautiful
new offices beside the quay. My host was a small elegant man
who walked with two sticks, and we ate in a glass dining room,
furnished with a sort of vivid restraint, overlooking the port
and the futuristic ships below. We ate alone. We were served
by an elderly Negro who also did the cooking, in a small
adjacent kitchen. The atmosphere was electronic, or perhaps
spatial. The luncheon was the very best meal I have ever
eaten in the United States of America.

One may imagine the impact of such sophisticated changes
upon that oldest of New York crafts, longshoremanship.
Here as everywhere, dockers are among the most conservative
and militant of workers, and nothing shocks them more than
a radical change in method. The last such major change was
the invention of the fork-lift truck, which transformed the
hoisting of things in and out of ships; but the arrival of the
container ship is far more drastic still.

Outside our window, as we discussed these matters after
lunch, the unloading of a ship proceeded. It was being
arranged by four fairly somnolent longshoremen and a single
crane driver in his gantry. Four more men were on board
the ship. Between them, with every sign of ease and indeed
of boredom, they lifted each container out of the hold, swung
it over the quay, and clicked it neatly into place upon the
waiting truck below. The truck drove away; another arrived;
the process was casually repeated; in a very few easy hours,
I was told, the job would be done.

"Sometimes," they said to me at the International Longshoremen's Association, "the working guy may prefer the
old ways, but that's the way the world goes." They said it
unconvincingly, though, for they clearly preferred the old

ways themselves. The first American longshoremen were part-timers, summoned from warehouses or even pastures when a ship came in, and their traditions have changed reluctantly ever since. Until the 1890s the Stars and Stripes was hoisted at the appropriate pier when a ship rounded Sandy Hook: "Flag's up!" went the cry, and down to the waterfront the longshoremen hastened, to be at the head of the queue for work. From early times they had been militants of society. They were a dangerous element, Lord Bryce wrote, wherever one found them in America. "Gentlemen and blackguards," cried the High Constable of New York to a crowd of dock strikers in 1836. "Go home or go along with me. 'Taint no way this to raise wages. If your employers won't give you your price, don't work: keep home and lay quiet. Make no riots here. I don't allow them things."

The reputation for violence has been especially lurid among the New York longshoremen, and in some periods their militancy has hamstrung the port. Their union affairs are extraordinarily complex, and shot through with internecine rivalries and inherited dislikes. I did not begin to master this confused situation. The very structure of the industry, even its terminology, is hard enough for a stranger to understand. In England, for instance, a stevedore is a dock laborer; in New York he is a contractor who provides labor. In England the man who actually works on a ship is a docker; in New York he is a longshoreman (short for an along-the-shore-man). In England one enormous union commands the intermittent loyalty of all dock workers. In New York the International Longshoremen's Association is divided into innumerable locals, each largely autonomous. The Holland-America terminal on Manhattan once embraced two piers, and accordingly still has two locals. Port Newark, on the other hand, only has two locals altogether, one white, one black. The ILA has often been divided in its top leadership, and for years its very name was synonymous with corruption and crime.

In the worst days of the New York waterfront—till the beginning of the 1950s, say—the complexity of the industry offered marvelous opportunities for graft. There were so many petty union bosses, each with patronage to offer or withhold. At the lowest level, local bosses demanded hard cash from longshoremen before they could get any work at all. Higher up the scale, union officials could blackmail steamship companies and stevedores by threatening to stop work, could place their crooked protégés in key positions all over the port, and could organize highly profitable systems of pilferage. Ex-convicts, in return for waterfront jobs, would be induced to undertake criminal assignments too. Rackets abounded, violence was commonplace.

In 1953 the New York Crime Commission reported that nearly a third of the local officials had criminal records. The daily "shape-up"—the hiring session at which longshoremen were offered work—was a notorious exchange of skulduggery and criminal intelligence. Among the senior officials of the ILA were Vincent "Cockeye" Brown, Joseph "Heels" Murphy, Anthony "Tony Cheese" Marchitto, and Frank "Machine Gun" Campbell of the Arsenal Mob, who disguised his own union authority by the use of other people's names, so that Mrs. Lucy Panzini, a Hoboken tavern proprietor, was distinctly surprised to be told one day that she was officially listed as president of Local 1478. There was, I need hardly say, not much democracy to this union. Elections were rare in the worst of the locals, and the ordinary longshoreman, often the rawest of unskilled immigrants, was as ruthlessly exploited by his own leaders as he was by the most implacable of the employers. All in all, the New York waterfront was a horrible mess. Shippers were reluctant to use so unsavory a harbor; many of the Manhattan piers were closed; neither the Government nor the shipping industry was anxious to invest money in the development of the port.

The New York newspapers exposed it all, and in 1954 the whole world learnt about it through the medium of the film *On the Waterfront,* starring Marlon Brando. Since then the port has been scoured with reforms. The ILA, when I spoke to its officers about the old evils, was at pains to assure me that they had been greatly exaggerated anyway. Its president, the celebrated Thomas ("Teddy") Gleason, welcomed me to his office with a courteous savoire-faire, rather as a gynecologist might receive a nervous patient, and gave me a book about his union inscribed "For a better understanding of our profession and union." "I want you," he said to an aide with a kindly smile in my direction—"I want you to show this visitor *everything.*"

We began at once, in the bar downstairs, where my chaperon had a couple of stiff whiskies in the half-light, and explained to me that things had never been as bad as they said. He had been on the waterfront all his life, and he could assure me that things had never been as bad as they said. They had always been very decent people down there, good Irish Catholics as often as not, who stood together like brothers. He had never—hardly ever—met a hoodlum during his years on the pier, and much of the unfortunate publicity the ILA had suffered was due to the activities of a waterfront priest, now fortunately transferred, whose sensationalism gave rise to *On the Waterfront* and all that. It had not been at all fair, my informant said, and that was why Mr. Gleason was anxious to present a more correct image of their profession and union to the world. If there was anything I wanted to see, anyone I wanted to talk to . . .

I felt rather like a hoodlum boss myself, as we swept

around the docks in the recesses of an immense Cadillac, which if not actually bullet-proof (it was only rented) smelt authentically, I thought, of Bourbon and cigars. The hiring hall we visited certainly seemed innocent enough. The hiring bosses looked almost genteel, and the longshoremen, told there was work at Hoboken or Brooklyn, stepped into their waiting cars rather as though they were off to the office (though in fact, since they are paid for the time they take in travelling to the piers, they often stop off for unnaturally long coffee breaks). It reminded me of Sotheby's, and was conducted, like that other earthy institution, with a certain ritual urgency. In the office a man was on the telephone, collating the needs of the port for labor that morning. "Okay, Jersey City wants twelve drivers, eight banana men. . . . Sure, I got a driver at Bayonne, where d'ya want him? . . . No, like I say, they don't want work in the hold. . . . Yeah, yeah, send him to Berth 7, ITO. . . . Whassat you say? Sure, category A, yeah. . . ."

Inside the hiring hall the four hiring bosses worked like auctioneers, offering jobs to the milling multi-racial blue-jowled crowd below. Sometimes they abruptly descended from one stand and mounted another: this was really because men of different categories are hired from different stands, but it looked as though the liturgy had been dictated by some forgotten Synod of the Waterfront. One or two middle-aged women secretaries wilted amid the the hubbub, and in general I found the performance disappointingly genteel. "See what I mean?" said my guide.

Many of the rank-and-file longshoremen still have criminal records, but today no convicted man can be an official of the union. A body called the Waterfront Commission of New York Harbor, part legal body, part police force, was set up in 1953 to clean up the waterfront and control the hiring of labor. This is a formidable institution. It was born out of public shock at the evidence of the Crime Commission inquiry, and out of the fear that the waterfront reputation would damage the port and the city. It was given extraordinary powers by its sponsors, the legislatures of New York and New Jersey: powers to screen all longshoremen, to dismiss them, to inquire into their past, to subpoena witnesses, to reform the whole system of dock hiring. It has opened a longshoremen's register. It has whittled down the labor force from some 50,000, many of them moonlighters, to 21,500 full-time workers. It claims to have elevated the moral tone of the docks: qualified longshoremen on the register now get a guaranteed quota of work—2,080 hours a year—with or without graft.

My friend from the ILA told me all this with melancholy resignation. The union detests the Waterfront Commission, which is known to longshoremen as the Gestapo, the N.K.V.D., or the Inquisition. What with this self-perpetuating agency battening upon the industry, and the advent of the container ships, my friend seemed to think, the whole future of the craft must be in doubt. The salty old days were gone for ever. The longshoremen were very nearly white-collar workers. "You call this a job for a grown man?" he demanded, waving a hand at the slow-moving workers beside a container ship. "Clean it may be, interesting it isn't." In ten years' time, he thought, the labor force would be halved. "See this gang here? There's sixteen men in that gang, but half of them have stayed home, there's not enough to do. They'll swap with these guys after the dinner break. D'you call that the dignity of labor?"

And as we drove back in our black limousine to Manhattan, and he talked to me about his own long life on the waterfront, the good guys and the worse, the years of fearful poverty and the long climb up to Mr. Gleason's elbow, I found myself unexpectedly warming to the longshoremen of New York. If their mayhem had been vicious, their fight for fair play had been full of pathos. Since the nineteenth century work on the docks had been pre-eminently the immigrants' trade: it was to the piers that the Irish and the Italians first made their way, unskilled, ignorant of the strange New World, without friends or cash, when they stepped off the Ellis Island ferry. Socially work on the docks was almost the bottom—in 1903 longshoring was ranked ninety-seventh in pay among the hundred chief nonprofessional occupations. Longshoremen found it impossible to get credit and often difficult to rent homes, and women were ashamed to own themselves wives of men on the waterfront. The Irish, who were there first, violently resented the arrival of the Italians, which added to the squalor of the scene: to this day the Manhattan piers are mostly worked by Irishmen, the Brooklyn piers by Italians.

For a century these people were mercilessly exploited: first by the employers, backed by officialdom, then by their own unscrupulous leaders. They lived generally in the slums that lined the waterfront, they earned miserable and irregular wages, they were vulnerable to every slump in trade, they were feared and despised by the public. The sailor was everyone's hero; the docker was a lout. My companion told me all about his own childhood on the docks, and his father's hard life upon the Manhattan piers. He spoke of his own particular pier, the pier he grew up on, as a man in other circumstances might speak of his old school; and he spoke of his union as of a defensive club, cap-a-pie against a hostile world, fighting for rights against the overwhelming odds of State and capitalism. I realized then that he was not being hypocritical, when he minimized the legend of waterfront brutality.

To him it was only incidental, only a disagreeable side issue, compared with the long struggle for a living wage and a place in society.

I do not say I accepted all he said, or saw his union and profession in quite the new image Mr. Gleason would prefer. The longshoremen are still among the more obstreperous of the city's workers, whose wildcat strikes and restrictive practices drive shipowners to distraction, and try the patience of the kindest captains. But after that day I did look at the longshoremen with more sympathy. My friend dropped me off at my hotel, where the porter, opening the Cadillac door for me, eyed me with an altogether new expression of mingled respect and suspicion; but I wandered down to the piers again that evening, and took a coffee and donut in a diner down there, and tried to imagine what it would have been like half a century ago, to be a poor Irishman plunged blind into this hard and dirty world along the shore. When the man on the next stool scowled across the napkin stand and said "Whassa matter wid you, you want all the sugar?" I told myself he was the victim of historical environment, and said I was most awfully sorry.

So many men along the waterfront—the pilots, the tugmen, the men from Wells Fargo, the immigration officers, the health officials, the Coast Guards, the customs men, the longshoremen—not to speak of the supporting forces behind, the customs brokers, the insurance men, the freight forwarders, the ship repairers, the coopers, the packers, the motor maintainers—so many wheels turning through the years, such an intricate, boisterous, instinctive process of portage! Let me end the chapter with a last tour around the port on a patrol boat of the Harbor Precinct, New York City Police, whose job it has been for a couple of hundred years to see that no grit is thrown into the machinery.

In the worst days of the longshoremen's thuggery, the waterfront of this port was a dangerous place. Nowadays the harbor areas seem, compared with the tensions of the inner city, reasonably harmless. Several security forces try to keep it so. There is a corps of watchmen who look after the piers themselves. There is a Port Authority police force. There are the Coast Guards and customs men. And down at Battery Point, sharing quarters with the fire service, are the men of the Harbor Precinct—who figured so determinedly, you may remember, in my earliest preconceptions of this port.

They live in the quaintest building on the whole waterfront—a comical little wooden structure with a tower, gimcrack and rickety, which survives miraculously among the downtown skyscrapers, the water of the harbor lapping its trestles, a smell of damp wood and old tobacco inside. Eight brisk police launches are perpetually on patrol in the harbor area—south to the Narrows, north to the city boundaries, and covering all the little islands of the archipelago. I remember my patrol with a languid, almost a holiday pleasure—like a watercolor of the harbor in my mind's eye, in which the ships on the Bay, the green islets, the workers on the waterfront, the channels and inlets, are disposed gracefully about the scene, unruffled.

Nothing whatever happened, as we chugged around the Manhattan circuit. All seemed to be in hand. The port was at work, the ships were on the move, the aircraft spun above the city, the three policemen on the boat chatted amiably and cleaned their rifles. Occasionally we paused to question the occupant of a junk-boat, plashing like a gray rodent beneath the piles of a quay, or make sure a small boy on a mudbank was not in fact about to drown, or check a lighter was safely moored, or sniff briefly around the luxuries of the 79th Street Boat Basin. Once we pulled in to a North River pier to telephone headquarters (leaving the radio waves free), and once we tied up beside an oil lighter, off the Fulton Fish Market, to take on diesel fuel.

I took out my notebook then, and recorded a small cameo —quintessential New York harbor: the two lean old Americans on the lighter, wearing peaked caps, smiling a little frostily, moving with a certain creaky elegance, and looking just like the Yankees Norman Rockwell used to dream up for the covers of the *Saturday Evening Post;* two workmen, talking loudly, being hoisted in a kind of bucket to the top of a half-demolished warehouse, where they emerged in silhouette with sledge hammers to continue the destruction; the masts and riggings of the fishing boats beside us, strung with nets and floats, with a little radar scanner twirling cheerfully in the sunshine; a big truck up there from the Knickerbocker Ice Company, its radiator muffled with canvas, a large supercilious seagull on top of its cab; the slow motion of the ships in the East River, against the backcloth of the Brooklyn bluffs; the thud of pile drivers, the clatter of a helicopter at the downtown heliport, the *basso profondo* of the traffic in the streets, the incomprehensible crackling murmur of the radio in the wheelhouse, the beat of the refueling pump, the click of the bolt as the policeman beside me greased his breech mechanism, and everywhere around us the perpetual glint of the New York waterfront—glint of water, of steel-sheathed buildings, of the scurrying cars on the expressway, glint of ships, of bridges, of boat gear, glint of sunshine, glint of metal shining out of the mud below, or blazing unexplained off the upper bay.

"No," says the sergeant as we cast off, "things are quieter these days on the harbor. What've we had, Joe? We had those crazy Cubans bombed the UN with mortar bombs from Brooklyn. What else? You get your dope peddlers. And your petty thieves."

"And your floaters," Joe says.

"Floaters! Well, I guess you get your floaters any place. I guess you have your floaters in London. Floaters is everywhere."

Chapter 10

CROSS-TOWN

"To move, move, move, as an end in itself, an appetite at any price." Once ashore, the energies of the port infect the city, which is in a condition of perpetual motion. New York has lived all its life upon innovation, and there never was a place of such mobility. The skaters on the ice at Rockefeller Center, in the heart of Manhattan, used to remind me of whirling atoms in the core of a reactor, spinning there night and day, summer or winter. Everything is done, if not with speed, at least with sweep. New York is seldom niggling. Even the chess players at the open-air tables in Washington Square move their pieces urgently, to a flow of badinage— "Be a gentleman! Look the other way!" Even the letter mail plummets from penthouse to basement in glass-fronted chutes. The lift was first perfected in England, but the precipitous elevators of New York long ago fostered a whole new body of peripatetic etiquette—"Out please," "Out 12," "Let the lady out," accompanied by a self-conscious removal of male hats and a kind of starched but fluttering simper peculiar to Manhattan secretaries on the move.

Many great cities, even seaports, give the impression of living for themselves, in comfort. They seem to sit there making things and using them, buying and exchanging among themselves, self-sufficient. Not New York. It is above all an open city, without walls, and it never was medieval. Its most celebrated characteristic has always been its sense of rush. It always appears to be going somewhere else, in one way, out another. The New Yorkers have neglected no device to speed up their own movements. They have tried, in their time, horse buses, sledge buses, hydrofoils, elevated railroads, cable cars and combination bus-trains. It is as though the ferocious momentum of the quays and the airports is pressing on their heels, and prodding them ever more relentlessly and uncomfortably from one place to another.

Yet it is often an inconclusive sort of motion. Journeys are generally only stages: taking a cargo from ship to shore to get it on a train, calling a cab to catch a helicopter to connect with a flight at JFK, boarding the Staten Island ferry to catch the subway at the Battery which will take you to Times Square for a cross-town bus to the United Nations. New York has always been renowned for its transient hotels. The City Hotel was grand enough in 1795, when its building at 115 Broadway was one of the most imposing in town; by 1842 Dickens was calling the St. Nicholas "the lordliest caravanserai in the world"; today the hotels of Manhattan, though mostly gruesome in one kind or another, are certainly myriad.

Part of the speckled or dappled quality of the place arises from the fact that the city is an archipelago. One cannot move far in New York without encountering a body of water, and the movement of small craft here and there across the rivers and creeks has always been essential to its character. Verrazano noticed the little boats, at the very beginning. Dickens thought them like "restless insects"—"laden with people, coaches, horses, waggons, baskets, boxes; crossed and re-crossed by other ferry-boats; all travelling to and fro; and never idle." "Thick as stars in the sky," was Walt Whitman's vision of them—"all sorts and sizes of sail and steam vessels, plying ferry-boats, arriving and departing coasters . . . with here and there, above all, those daring, careening things of grace and wonder, those white and shaded swift-darting fish-birds—first-class New York sloop or schooner yachts."

For 250 years New York was a city of ferries. The very first was established in the 1630s to provide a service between Manhattan and Brooklyn; in 1806, Cornelius Vanderbilt started the Staten Island ferry that was the basis of an immense New York fortune; by the end of the nineteenth century the double-ended steam ferry, with its high funnels and fluttering flags, was among the most familiar of New York spectacles. In 1908 there were 38 ferry services here and there across the archipelago, chuffing and hooting indefatigably, sometimes all night. A grand camaraderie bound the ferry crews, a sentimental loyalty the passengers. In 1907 a famous race took place between two ferryboats of the Erie and Lackawanna Railroad. The course was from Hoboken to Newburgh, New York, and back—some 60 miles—and it was accomplished, so the newspapers of the day tell us, with majestic splashing of paddles and belching of black smoke, in a winning time of a little less than seven hours. "Thousands who travel daily on the two boats," as the New York *Observer* remarked, "little realize that they are capable of going faster than the average battleship." During the First World War soldiers arriving in New York from the Middle West, *en route* to Europe, sometimes assumed the towering and haughty ferryboats to be their transatlantic transports.

The only remaining public ferry services are those to Hart Island, Liberty Island, and Staten Island; and of these only the last, directly descended from Vanderbilt's line, is a ferry in the old rumbustious sense. Its 24 boats do not bear much physical resemblance to the classic steamboats of the past, but they are fine big diesel craft, painted violently, as they should be, and given names like *American Legion II, Governor Herbert H. Lehman,* or *Miss New York.* They belong to the City of New York, and fly the City flag beside the Stars and Stripes; the newest can carry 3,000 passengers and 40 vehicles at 18 knots across the Bay. They make a splendid sight still, especially in the dark, when their lights move swiftly and powerfully across the harbor; and they command, even now, the traditional loyalty of the ferryboat passengers, who make a fearful fuss whenever it is proposed to raise the legendary nickel fare, or reduce the all-night service.

Side by side with them, what is more, as they slide into their modern terminal at South Ferry, two private ferries of a different character still plod in and out of a very different ferry station. These are the old boats that go to Governors Island. They are all one could ask of a New York ferry—tall-funneled, very upright, old and creaky, with the pilot high in a gazebo at his enormous wheel, and old mahogany staircases inside, and lattice seats; and when they have pottered across the hundred yards or so of their voyage, they subside into a proper old-school ferry terminal. Its three cavernous bays are plunged in shadow and surrounded by flamboyant ironwork, and the boats seem to collapse into their waiting slips—with a colossal groaning of teak piles, with a grinding of planks and a racing of engines, as the old iron gangplanks are lowered out of the rafters to the upper deck, and the dirty water heaves and eddies in the half-light.

Here and there around the Bay you may see other such memorials of the ferry age—palatial half-derelict stations on the New Jersey shore, or smelly old termini of Manhattan, ingrained with dirt and smoke. Most of them are relics of railroad ferry service, connecting Manhattan with railheads on the New Jersey shore, and they are all deserted now. The last railroad ferry of all, the Erie-Lackawanna ferry between Manhattan and Hoboken, ran its last voyage when I was in New York, and never I imagine was there a more authentically New York occasion. Mourners and celebrators packed the dismal old Manhattan terminal (40-watt bulbs, overflowing litter bins, the clock stopped at ten to three): newspapermen, cameramen, roistering office workers, people with banners and leaflets and comic hats and crates of champagne, a trio of Salvation Army girls singing unaccompanied holy songs indefatigably above the noise. I sat down on a grubby bench between two elderly habitués of the ferry. "He's doing all right," said one of the other, when I inquired if the noise wasn't too much for him, "he's seventy-eight years old, and he's doing all right, God bless him."

"You sound kinda British," the old man then said himself. "Funny place for you to be, ain't it? You ride this boat regular?"

"Never before in my life," said I.

"Well, you don't say. Some people have it easy. I've had to ride this ferry forty years to make the last crossing. You come over and do it first time!"

And when the dowdy old boat came in at last, and we crowded aboard her in the darkness, what a half-forgotten New York, innocent and high-spirited, came to life under her influence! The Hoboken High School band, in scarlet with white-feathered helmets, played lustily in the bows. Streamers fluttered. Corks popped. Somebody shouted "Ferry Power!" To a great cheer and a blowing of sirens, echoing from vessel to vessel along the Hudson, the Erie Lackawanna ferry set off on her last voyage. She moved very slowly, wallowing, and as we labored across the stream the Hoboken High School band broke into "Auld Lang Syne." A maudlin excitement seized us then. There was a wild laughing rush for the life jackets, until everybody was festooned with bright red, and some people were wearing four or five. The old engines hissed, the sirens hooted, "Auld Lang Syne" rang raggedly through the night, and with a great cheer we bumped our way into the dim pillared labyrinth of the Erie-Lackawanna Railroad and Ferry Station, Hoboken, New Jersey. It was all over.

I had arranged to be picked up by a helicopter on the New Jersey side, and presently I was out at JFK, where I was catching a jet to Europe.

The ferries were injured by the bridges of New York, but it was the tunnels that ruined them. Many underwater tunnels now connect Manhattan with the mainland and the rest of the archipelago—four road tunnels, two railroad tunnels, numerous subway tunnels. They will never match the ferries for picturesque allure, if only because they begin unobtrusively, almost surreptitiously, on the edge of Manhattan—obscure holes in the ground into which the traffic seems to sidle shamefaced. Once I realized how many there were, though, and accustomed my mind to the millions of people and hundreds of thousands of vehicles that plunge into them each day, to pass beneath the ships to the other shore, then they too began to color my view of New York, and gave me a queer sensation of a city with secret entrances and exits, like corridors beneath a castle moat.

The most exciting of them is the Lincoln Tunnel, which is run by the Port Authority, and was opened in 1937. Its three tubes go underground near West 38th Street in Manhattan, and emerge on the New Jersey shore in a spiral of approach roads, climbing to the crest of the Weehawken ridge with a spectacular farewell view of the Manhattan towers behind. This is probably the busiest tunnel in the world, at least 83,000 vehicles passing through it every day, and a work force of some 350 makes sure it never closes. They also make sure it pays its way. I remarked to a tunnel man one day that profit, or at least solvency, seemed to play a surprisingly large part in the thinking of the organization, essentially a social service after all. "Oh, don't get us wrong," he said, "it's the people component that counts."

The people component can be seen at its most alarming during the evening rush hour, when the commuters pour off Manhattan Island through the tunnel. For the tunnel men this is the climax of the day—the moment when the balance of traffic shifts, and the center tube of the three must be changed from two-way to west-bound flow. Tension builds up in the early evening, as the police controllers in their glass box at the Jersey end ("the Dairy Queen") keep their eye on the mounting traffic. Gradually, as the darkness begins to fall, the traffic thickens, until the television cameras in the tube are never without a car on screen, and the flow is solid. "We're picking 'em up on the city streets now," says the controller. "They're backing up into Ninth Avenue, up to 34th or 35th Street."

Now the big commuter buses stream out of the tube, one after the other, gleaming in the toll-booth lights, and now quite suddenly there seem to be cars everywhere, a milling mass of cars at the tunnel mouth, cars nose to tail, cars crawling, cars flashing without pause in and out of the television screens. The flow of vehicles is controlled electronically, and the press of a button opens or closes an approach lane, or halts everything to allow the yellow breakdown truck, with a theatrical roar of its engines, to swing out of its yard and race into the tube.

"Building up for the shift now," says the controller, "traffic's backing way up into the midtown streets"—and he presses a button on his panel. At once the east-bound lane of the central tube is blocked, and traffic is diverted to the next tube. The toll girls in their cabins shift booths; a policeman moves the traffic barriers. A long pause follows, as that single lane remains unnaturally abandoned in the mêlée, and then a police jeep emerges with flashing lights out of the tunnel. The way is clear. It is like uncorking champagne. Immediately the traffic gushes out behind, as though it has been bottled up there all day, and the full tide of the people component pours out of Manhattan and streams away over the ridge to supper. "Of course," my informant had told me, "things are different on Sundays. Historically it's only private traffic on Sunday."

"Fewer commuter units?"

"That's right," he said approvingly. I was getting the hang of things.

In a subway station one day I struck up a conversation with the lady at the ticket booth, who worked deep underground at the platform entrance, and was protected against hooligans by a thick metal grille. Let me set the scene of our meeting. The station was excavated in the early days of the New York subway system, and suggests a particularly cramped and airless cave, or perhaps a sunken submarine. Its tubes are very narrow. Its platforms are inexplicably long, and echo. It feels as though there is not quite enough air to breathe easily, so that life is only sustained by hidden pumps and air shafts. It makes you feel you want to put on your escape apparatus, and climb out through the hatch. When I was there that morning the place was deserted except for a solitary Negro, who sat slumped upon a seat in an attitude of incurable dejection, occasionally springing to his feet in a jerky sort of way and walking a few feet along the platform, his footsteps echoing. There was no suggestion of a train. The station seemed altogether sufficient to itself, altogether cut off from the busy life of the city far above, like a setting for Brecht.

The lady at the booth was elderly, and all white. Her hair was white. Her face was ashen. Her eyes seemed to have no pupils. It was as though she had never in her life emerged into the daylight, but had been born and bred in that subterranean gloom. When I asked her how she liked working down there, and whether she did not miss the sun, she was rather affronted. What could I know about it? She had worked in the subway for thirty years, and did not regret a moment of it. She loved the old station, liked to see the trains go by, and had many friends among the passengers; and sure enough, when a more protracted spasm than usual sent the Negro within speaking range, he called out unexpectedly to that white lady behind her grille: "Howya doin', ma'am? Keepin' well?" "I'm fine, Jack, thank you kindly," she replied, "keepin' just fine."

So there is a sort of catacomb tradition to the subways of New York. The people at the Port Authority, who reluctantly took over one bankrupt line in 1962, told me that loyalty among its employees was fervent: their average age was high, and they had mostly been with the company man and boy for ever. I wish I could report the same family pride among the users of the New York subways, but in fact nobody I met had a good word to say for them. Half a century ago the system was the pride of the city, and innumerable photographs and Special Artists' drawings portray ceremonial opening journeys, with bigwigs of all sorts holding their top hats on their knees and looking distinctly apprehensive as they are whisked by the modern marvel of the subway from one beflagged terminal to another.

The building of the first underground railway in New York was delayed for years because of political pressure from "Boss" Tweed of Tammany, who ran the buses. The first subway was accordingly disguised as a pneumatic mail tube: it ran for a single block, under Broadway from Murray Street to Warren Street, and it had a waiting room almost half as long as the line, equipped with a grand piano, a goldfish tank, and a fountain. In 1904 the first publicly owned subway was opened, causing so much excitement that according to the New York *World* men fought each other to get tickets. "Women were dragged out, either screaming in hysterics or in a swooning condition: gray-headed men pleaded for mercy, boys were knocked down and only escaped by a miracle from being trampled underfoot."

The system rapidly spread, and the dignitaries took their walking sticks to opening after opening, as the lines spread northwards into the Bronx, under the East River to Brooklyn, under the Hudson to the New Jersey shore. Then, between the two world wars, it stuck. Shuffled from public to private ownership, and back again to public, the subway system has been generally stagnant for thirty years. The Port Authority has done something to rejuvenate its own line, PATH, equipping it with smart new rolling stock and jollying up its stations one by one; for the rest the sepulchral tunnels of the New York subway still bear the patina of a generation's misery.

They say it is the biggest underground system in the world. Certainly it is in some ways the most spectacular, even now. There are places under Manhattan where several lines coincide on different levels, and enormous city-like warrens have been excavated down there, complete with shops and restaurants; and you may walk it seems for miles along the corridors, ablaze with light, up and down stairs, in and out of vaulted arcades, from one musty platform to another. The New York underground is not much concerned to guide the stranger through its mazes. System maps are almost totally incomprehensible, there are few of the illuminated signs and

colored lights which comfort the visitor to gentler tubes, and
the innocent who ventures to ask for help may get some
frank replies, like "How the hell do I know?" or "Can't you
read the signs?" As the editors of Michelin's New York guide
discreetly put it: "Riding the New York subway is an
exciting experience for visitors, but daily commuters who
have had a chance to try the comforts of the Paris or
Montreal metros would probably prefer to ride on those silent
and modern trains equipped with special steel cord tires of
French manufacture."

But exciting, yes. Most of the subway trains seem to travel
at about a hundred miles an hour, and they sway and rattle
thrillingly through the tunnels, and stop in the stations with
violent hissing noises. During the rush hours they are so
crowded that a man can hardly shift his elbow without being
suspected of improper behavior. At other times they are
ominously empty, and at night every train is patrolled by
an armed policeman, strolling up and down the swaying
carriages swinging his night stick and whistling through his
teeth.

A ghastly hush hangs like a fog in the subway stations,
between trains. Across the dark chasm of the tracks the
people on the opposite platform look unnaturally vivid,
framed there between the platform pillars as in a polyptych,
and funereally illuminated. Slumped on benches, propped
against walls the travelers wait, unsmiling, and in front of
them all, perhaps, a solitary girl in high boots walks slowly
down the platform, swaying her umbrella on a strap. Snatches
of low-voiced conversation reach you: "I told him, I said
Johnnie, if you want me you've just gotta come right down
to the Village and get me." . . . "Crooked? Crooked as a
snake, I tell you, crooked as a green snake." . . . "She said
that? She actually said that, right there? She said that to your
face?" . . . "Listen Ed, I'll blind you, honest I will, I'll cut

your tongue out you old son of a gun you." . . . "Listen,
who d'ya take me for? Think I'm the company or sump'n?
Can't you read the signs?"

And then with a whoosh and a clatter the train comes in,
and all those vagrant souls are swept away to another limbo
along the line.

For me the All-American has always been the Manhattan
bus driver. Since long ago I first saw his weary, slightly
bitter, preoccupied face above the wheel—since I first saw
him clicking that little lever on his change machine, to the
tinkle of the dimes and nickels sorting themselves out—since
I first heard his timeless response: "Yeah, lady, get out at
41st Street"—since I first plucked up courage to ask him if
he could manage change for a ten-dollar bill—ever since I
first made his acquaintance, he has exemplified for me that
New Man, the American. He works as hard as a New Man
should, not merely conducting the bus, but answering questions as he drives, cursing cab drivers, even making occasional
passes at transient birds. Then again the look of him is very
American: not his face so much, which may vary from the
Slav to the Negro, but his slumped shirt-sleeved posture
over the wheel, the disillusioned slump of him, the weary
reach of his arm towards the change machine—all the
hallmarks of a man who has seen the world, knows New
York to be its epitome, and has no illusions about the place.
"So it's a big city? Sure it is. So they're tall buildings? So?"

The first horse-drawn bus ran in New York, and Victorian
visitors to the city often admired the resplendent panache of
the bus services: the Red Bird Line, the Yellow Bird Line,
the Original Broadways. The motorbuses, though, seem to
have lost their confidence under the assault of the private
car, so that they now move with lurching diffidence through
the traffic, when they really ought to be in command. New

York gave up double-decker buses soon after the Second World War, and the bus service is now sadly limited. The city buses stick to a few obvious routes, up and down the avenues, across one or two cross-town streets, and do not pretend to provide a comprehensive service. The Manhattan service is desperately slow: it begins and ends well enough, in the open streets at the top and bottom of the island, but there comes a time in the middle of every daytime journey when the frantic traffic of the mid-town business section slows your bus almost to a walking pace, and a glazed look overcomes the faces of the patient passengers, and the slump of the driver's shoulders becomes more fatalistic than ever. The bus as a method of rapid transit in Manhattan has lost its chance: often it is literally quicker to walk.

But as a means of getting off the island, the bus is now in its heyday. New York's biggest bus terminal, the Port Authority terminal on Eighth Avenue, is in fact the busiest passenger terminal of any kind anywhere, handling more passengers every day than any railroad station, dock, or airport. So familiar a part does it play in the life of Manhattan that if you hail a cab and say simply "Port of Authority," the bus terminal is where you will go. Well over 200,000 people use it every day, 65 million a year; but not all are travelers, for it has long been a place of casual resort, a haven for idlers, a rendezvous for lovers, and a promenade for voyeurs and romantics of all sorts. It is like a grand piazza of movement, into which the passers-by are dragged by sheer centripetal force.

Here better than anywhere else you may sense the stepping-stone function of New York, the function of transfer or relay. The terminal occupies an entire city block, and is less a temple of movement, as the old railroad terminals wished to be, than a caravanserai. It has its own dentist, physician, pediatrist, health-food store, religious-articles store, music store, and bowling alley. Hidden away in a kind of bunker, perpetually locked against criminal entry, a corps of women operators, day and night, deals with inquiries, timed by watchful supervisors to keep them on the mark. Forty escalators crawl from floor to floor, and 7,500 buses drive in and out each day, rumbling from the three loading decks direct into the Lincoln Tunnel under the river. Almost all the west-bound bus traffic of New York begins at this terminal, the separate bus companies having been assembled over the years under its one cavernous roof.

Here you may see many a classic stereotype of Manhattan, familiar to all the world from movie or musical: the small-town girl arriving to try her luck, rather too heavily made up, with her vanity bag and squashy-topped suitcase; the homely folk from Michigan or Indiana, returning home with relief after a week with their suave physician son and the snooty wife he met at Columbia; the servicemen, whooping it into town at the start of a furlough, or clambering limply into their bus, rings around their eyes, after the long weekend.

One after the other in a constant stream, the gleaming buses trundle down their ramps into the tunnel. The people who run the terminal assured me, when we discussed the problems of congestion and expansion, that "you can do more with buses than you can with people"—buses being foreseeable, tractable, and on wheels. Their terminal, though, is above all a place of human excitement. There has been at least one childbirth inside it, and at least one murder. Sometimes it reminds me of a London subway during an air raid, when one saw one's fellow citizens stripped for the first time of artificial distinction, and elevated to a common denominator; and sometimes the bus terminal suggests Russia, in its force of numbers, in its human richness, and its ageless rolling rhythm.

But of all the devices by which the New Yorkers have assuaged their restless urges, much the most splendid are the bridges. I agree with V. S. Pritchett, who says in his *New York Proclaimed* that these are the finest things the New Yorker has ever made—"architecturally it is the bridges rather than the buildings or even the way of life that are the supreme American achievement." For the lover of bridges, this is the ultimate city. If Venice and Amsterdam have more, if San Francisco possesses one arguably more thrilling, if Isfahan and Florence have more peculiar examples, if Sydney is more theatrically dominated by a single bridge, and Paris more absolutely by a dozen, still New York is richer in noble bridges than any other city in the world.

This is a gift of the archipelago. Bridges are everywhere around this Bay, their towers and latticeworks looming at the ends of streets, their suspension wires foreshortened by perspective, so that the three East River bridges sometimes seem to be all in a tangle of steel wire and stanchion. Over Newark Bay the hump-back of the Bayonne Bridge stands in massive silhouette, and far up towards Long Island Sound the towers of the suspension bridges are scattered inexplicably across the landscape, in places where no water seems to be. I was taken by a friend one evening to a secluded spot on the north shore of Long Island where Manhasset Bay debouches into the Sound. We were twenty miles from Manhattan, but on the horizon the towers stood mauve and massive in the evening, and the first city lights shone, and the jets rode their vapor trails into the sky from La Guardia. Above the muddled mass of the city buildings, north of the skyscrapers, I could see two square pylons, looking squat, hefty, and rather Egyptian. For me they stole the scene, half hidden as they were, and hard enough to see, for they were the towers of the George Washington Bridge, on the

other side of Manhattan Island, far far away across the
Bronx: like distant temple towers, over a desert.

Sometimes I walked across Brooklyn Bridge, if the morning
was fine enough, and I was in a bridge mood. There is a
boardwalk across it, in the center of the span, and there the
pedestrian has a breezy sense of supremacy, as he strides across
the planking in the morning sun, the cars out of sight below
him, and silenced by the wind, the East River opening away
into the grand expanse of the upper bay. Cranks of one sort
or another appear to make most use of this fine promenade,
to my mind the best walk in Manhattan. One sees fresh-air
fanatics parading there, breathing rhythmically; one sees
dedicated history buffs nosing their way across in groups,
observing only windjammers where the expressways run, and
looking hard for Union Jacks above Governors Island; one
sees scowl-faced shambling solitaries whose hobbies do not
bear thinking about; one sees self-satisfied foreigners with
notebooks, looking as though they owned the harbor, and
staring with patronizing calculation at every passer-by.

Brooklyn Bridge was the first, and is still the most famous,
of the great New York suspension bridges. "Where's Brooklyn?" asked a sophisticated New Yorker in a Hollywood
comedy of the 1940s, and the reply was only half a joke:
"I think you take a bridge to get there." This was the first
steel cable suspension bridge. It caught the imagination of
the world from the start, and its origins were made romantic
by tragedy: its designer, the German John Roebling, was
injured by a ferryboat during the work, and died of tetanus;
his son Washington, who took over, collapsed while working
in a pneumatic caisson, and was paralyzed for life. The bridge
was opened in 1883, the celebratory parade making a detour
to Roebling's house, to pay tribute to the invalid engineer.
It remained for twenty years the longest suspension bridge

in the world. Every foreign visitor marveled at it (except the grumpy Sir Lepel Griffin, author of *The Great Republic*, who inspected it shortly before its opening, and described it only as "an instance of what swindling on a gigantic scale is able to accomplish"). H. G. Wells thought it far more impressive than the skyscrapers, with its Cyclopean stone arches and its long sweep "far up in one's sky." Walt Whitman was inspired by its "grand obelisk-like towers . . . giant brothers twain." Hart Crane apostrophized it:

> O *harp and altar, of the fury fused,*
> (*How could mere toil align thy choiring strings!*) . . .

Brooklyn Bridge was a technical phenomenon. Many of its innovations—notably the use of steel cables and the manner of passing them across the river—have never been superseded: every other New York suspension bridge is recognizably descended from this magnificent old stalwart.

On the other shore of Manhattan stands the George Washington Bridge, in its time, too, the longest in the world. This is a much nobler thing. It stands very high above a much more splendid river, and is embedded at its western end in the wooded bluffs of the Palisades—a very different conclusion from the homely clutter of Brooklyn. Of all the bridges I know, this is the most plutocratic, bearing about it all the hallmarks of success. It is a masterpiece of strength and function, with its fourteen lanes on two decks, the vast solidity of its towers, and the impression it gives of having rammed itself irresistibly into the New Jersey shore. The bridge was opened in 1931: in 1963 the Port Authority, which operates it, added a bus station at the eastern end, forming an integral part of the bridge, and invited Pier Nervi to design a roof for it. This commission Nervi fulfilled in an unexpected way, capping a new whirl of approach

roads with the neatest and merriest bus station you ever saw—
a graceful concrete structure with a roof like the wings of
stylized pigeons.

Throughout the twentieth century bridges have been pro-
liferating across the New York waterways—seven more
bridges across the East River, two across the Arthur Kill,
a turnpike bridge over Newark Bay, bridges across Jamaica
Bay and Rockaway Inlet and Bowery Bay and innumerable
lesser inlets. Until 1964, however, the grandest space of all
waited to be spanned. Perhaps the most wonderful site for a
bridge in the world is the entrance to New York harbor, the
Narrows, the supreme gateway of the Americas. For half a
century the New Yorkers had talked of bridging this gap,
to connect Staten Island with Brooklyn and Manhattan. There
had been a plan for a railroad tunnel under the Narrows;
in 1923 the Mayor of New York had actually broken ground
for a road tunnel; for twenty years at least they had con-
templated a bridge. The real-estate men had pressed for it.
The military opposed it. The conservationists argued for the
pristine nature of Staten Island. The politicians politicked. It
was not until 1959 that a decision was reached at last, and the
bridge was built.

This is now the longest suspension bridge, and perhaps
the loveliest. Many people wish it had never been built—
"never again," Mr. Pritchett mourns, "shall we experience
that mysterious doubt as to the exact moment when we
entered into the open sea or came into the haven." Not me.
I like the moment to be explicit, and for me the glory of
the Narrows bridge is precisely that: neither its soaring grace,
nor its setting, but its effect. It has made a lagoon of the
upper bay, and given to all the creeks, kills, and waterways,
all the expressways of the city, all the lesser bridges, all the
tugs and ferries and littered islands, a new organic unity. The

cars streaming across the Narrows today seem to close a last circuit in the electricity of New York.

I was moved by these great bridges, and they came to exemplify for me the ambiguities of the city—colossal assurance in their construction, uncertainty and anxiety in the swarm of their nightmare traffic. When I began to inquire into their history, I found to my astonishment that one man seemed to have built half of them, and was thus in a sense the creator of the New York we know. O. H. Ammann was born in Switzerland in 1879, and had come to America in his twenties. Before he died in 1964 he had played a leading part in the design or construction of at least nine big New York bridges: the Outerbridge Crossing, the Bayonne Bridge, the Triborough Bridge, the Hell Gate Bridge, the Bronx-Whitestone Bridge, the Goethals Bridge, the George Washington Bridge, the Throgs Neck Bridge, and at last that final *tour de force* across the Narrows. Several of these works were entirely his: he designed them, he made them; no builder in history has left a grander memorial.

I asked everybody about this man, and was given cautious assessments. Many people found him daunting. "A stiff, formal Swiss gentleman," said Gay Talese in his book *The Bridge*, "well-born and distant." Mr. Tobin remembered him with respect and affection, but agreed he was hardly a man for intimacies. He was the kind of man who never called you by your first name, but he was immensely admired by his workmen. There was a bust of him in Nervi's bus station, and when I looked at his bridges I often used to imagine his spare and rigid figure inspecting them too, familiar with every stress and girder. I was told he had loved the George Washington Bridge, in particular, like a child.

In the end I pursued his memory to his last home, an air-conditioned house in Westchester County, with big windows overlooking open country behind. There his widow fed me handsomely on raw beef and salad, and there I got to know him. He was not at all, I think, the severe and unimpassioned aristocrat so many New Yorkers had found him. He was one of the grand romantics. We looked at his books and his trophies there, we saw an early photograph of him, more like a poet than a technician, soft-eyed and dreaming during his first years in New York. We saw the fine old iron gate he had brought from his family home in Switzerland, and the coppice next door he had acquired simply to have somewhere for the gate to open into. The house was full of signs of his great bridges, preliminary penciled sketches, plans, pictures, mementoes; and I got the impression as we talked of a man whose professional eminence hid from people an intense emotional activity. Ammann did not like city life. Gregarious bonhomie was not to his taste, and as often as he could he withdrew to that quiet comfortable house in the country—country as ordered and as green as Switzerland itself. He believed in experience. At sixty-five he retired from the Port Authority to set up his own firm, and to it came many distinguished engineers, when they too reached retiring age elsewhere. He himself was in his eightieth year when he started work on the Narrows bridge.

I can see that this reticent nonconformist must sometimes have seemed a cold fish, in the overheated Martini pool of Manhattan. But I thought of him often later in his apartment on the twenty-seventh floor of the Hotel Carlyle, on East 76th Street in Manhattan, where he lived when he was on the job. From there, Mrs. Ammann told me, he could see several of his great bridges, around the horizons of the Bay; and often he used to sit up there at his window alone, looking at them through a telescope.

Chapter 11

TO THE HINTERLAND

The *bevorland* of New York is the Atlantic. The hinterland is the whole land mass of North America, and from this port substances and conceptions are pumped out, like life-blood, throughout the arteries of the United States. New York very early saw itself as a metropolis, destined to overtake the hoarier cities of the seaboard, and in the 1790s Talleyrand agreed: "Its good and convenient harbor, which is never closed by ice, and its central position, to which large rivers bring the products of the whole country, appear to me to be decisive advantages. Philadelphia is too buried in the land and especially too inaccessible to wood of all sorts. . . . Boston is too much at the extremity of the country. . . ." Before the end of the eighteenth century New York was already described as "a sort of Mecca to the hungry back-woodsman, who was sure to make a pilgrimage once in his lifetime to yield his homage on its counters." For five years, between 1785 and 1790, New York was actually the capital of the United States; since the 1830s it has been the biggest city.

These truisms are most expressively illustrated by the railroad lines. From a helicopter you may see them streaming down to New York out of the interior: southward down the Hudson shore, northward through Bayonne, across Staten Island to Saint George. As they approach the waters of the Bay they proliferate into marshaling yards, sidetracks, and depots, and are projected into finger piers; fleets of tugs and scows hang about, ready to relieve them of their burdens, and everywhere across the harbor you may see the floating railroad cars, apparently axle-deep in the effluence of the Bay, whose movement from hinterland to waterfront is one of the most characteristic sights of this port.

The economic watershed of New York is almost immeasurable, so unique is the place the city occupies in national life. Within the metropolitan region itself lives nearly 9 per cent of the population of the United States; though this proportion is declining, as undeveloped regions of the country expand, the population itself is going up, so that by the year 2000, it is projected, some 30 million people will live within 60 miles of the harbor—one out of every 200 people on earth. This region in itself is enough to offer any port a living, and the metropolitan area provides New York with the same kind of immediate source and market as the Low Countries provide Rotterdam. But like Rotterdam, New York has far greater interests. It has long aspired to be a continental port, and it competes vigorously for custom as far inland as Chicago and Saint Louis.

Its original hinterland was the South, in the days when the "cotton triangle" secured for New York almost a monopoly of the Southern trade. Southern merchants deeply resented this success. The South was "feeding from her own bosom," declared one manifesto of protest, "a vast population of merchants, shipowners, capitalists and others, who . . . drink up the life-blood of her trade." It was an early example of dollar imperialism—capturing the business without assuming the responsibilities—and like other imperialisms is having its aftereffects now, as the Negroes of the South crowd into New York in search of fair shares and fulfillment.

It was still a sea trade—most of the merchandise was carried in coastal shipping. What first turned an Atlantic settlement into a continental gateway was the Erie Canal, a waterway connecting the Hudson River with the Great Lakes and so the whole of the American West. This was one of the great engineering feats of the nineteenth century—in its social and historical meaning, arguably the greatest of all. In the early days of American expansion the rich lands of the West were cut off from the sea by the Appalachian Mountains, which extend from Maine to Louisiana, and could be crossed in those days only by appalling exertions of oxcart and snowshoe. The only economic way of exporting the wheat of the Middle West was to load it on scows and sail it down the Mississippi to New Orleans; even then the profits were low, and most of the Western settlers did not bother to sell their wheat, but merely lived at a subsistence level, eating it themselves.

"The Big Ditch," 350 miles long through an unmapped wilderness, was intended not merely to connect these great new areas of resource with their markets, but specifically to channel all their produce through the port of New York. It was a colossal promotion job. The canal took eight years to cut, the dirtiest work being done, we are told, by "wild bog trotters from Western Ireland," and in 1825 a triumphal procession of boats made an inaugural journey from Buffalo, beside the Niagara Falls, into New York Bay. Cannon stationed along the route signaled the progress of the armada, and small boats and river steamers joined it along the way; until at last Governor Clinton of New York State, on board the *Seneca Chief,* led a flotilla of twenty-nine steamboats and hundreds of sailing craft down the Hudson into New York. "Whence come you," hailed the city fathers self-consciously, from the steamer *Washington,* "and where are you bound?" "From Lake Erie," the *Seneca Chief* replied, "bound for Sandy Hook!" Flags flew all over New York as the fleet sailed past Manhattan; the crew of a British warship very decently lined their decks and cheered; and when the *Seneca Chief,* passing through the Narrows to applause from both banks, reached the open Atlantic at Sandy Hook, Governor Clinton poured into the ocean a cask of water from Lake Erie. It was like the annual wedding of Venice and the Adriatic, except that here there was a marriage broker: the West was espoused to the wide world indeed, but New York had made the arrangements.

Now New York really did become a continental port, and the growing Middle West looked to Manhattan as its chief outlet to the world. All along the Erie Canal new towns sprang up, all protégés of New York, all to become in time importers and exporters through the port. Wheat, pork, rye whisky poured in an ever-growing stream eastwards to the Bay—as early as 1826 nineteen thousand boats passed by one town on the canal—and all the comforts of the industrial revolution, buggies to Lancashire calico, sailed to the West from the marts of New York. The Great Lakes themselves became part of the New York system of waterways, and the Hudson River turned out to be, as Hudson had surmised, a kind of Northwest Passage after all.

Today there is not much water traffic from New York to the Great Lakes, though the canal is still navigable. Ocean-going ships still sail up the Hudson to Albany, but nothing bigger than a barge goes west. The St. Lawrence Seaway takes the sea traffic now. Even the splendid river liners that used to sail from New York up the Hudson, with their pillared, chandeliered, and verandaed saloons, their gigantic house flags, their resident orchestras, and their gas lighting— all are gone, to be succeeded only by the modest excursion boats that sail in the summer months decorously up to West Point and Bear Mountain.

Yet New York remains the chief Atlantic outlet for the American Middle West. The Port Authority works hard to keep it so, having its own office in Chicago, but perhaps it is largely a matter of habit. Today ships can sail direct from Chicago down the Seaway to the Atlantic; but the big trunk railways, the real sinews of inland America, still converge most massively upon New York. During the First World War, when the port was paralyzed by the volume of traffic, railroad rolling stock was backed up immobile in sidings and marshaling yards all the way to Pittsburgh: so intimate is the connection between this particular waterfront and the great cities of the West.

There are places in New York where, looking through grilles in the sidewalk, one may see the coaches of big trains slinking through the darkness underneath. I liked the sense of clandestine communication given by this spectacle. So did Thomas Wolfe, who used to sit at night and listen to the rumble of the trains below, coming and going from Grand Central Station. Although Manhattan has risen with the rise of the railroads, and supported the fortunes of more than one railway mogul, it has been reticent about its trains. This is partly because the first line to run into Manhattan came from the north—the New York Central, which gave the Vanderbilts their fortune. Its approach, down the line of the island rather than across its rivers, was unobtrusive, and the terms of its monopoly decreed that no other railway could enter the island except by tunnel. None did until 1912, when the Pennsylvania Railroad emerged blinking from beneath the Hudson River into Pennsylvania Station. To this day no proud expresses storm through the island, with the clanking of bells and shattering rumble of diesels that attend American trains elsewhere: most visitors to Manhattan never see a train at all.

Nevertheless the two great railroad termini of the island demonstrate the old consequence of railway interests in Manhattan. Both were conceived on a scale more lavish and confident than anything on the waterfront—more akin to the airports than the docks. Pennsylvania Station has been razed to make way for the new Madison Square Garden, and has been replaced by an underground depot of clinical modernity, but in its great days it was one of the show places of New York. It was based upon the Emperor Caracalla's baths in Rome, and was lined with Doric columns, and lit by enormous skylights, and guarded by six great stone eagles above the portico. As for Grand Central, the terminus of the New York Central line, it remains the grandest New York memorial to the age of plush and feathers. It was completed in 1913, to serve both the New York Central and the New York, New Haven lines from the north, and it is radiant still with decorous pomp. The trains are hidden away below ground, and the immense concourse above is conceived on the scale, and in the manner, of a cathedral. Although hundreds of thousands of people jostle through this place each day, still the uniformed officials of Grand Central retain something of the aloof dignity of vergers, and at quiet moments the very echo of one's feet across the vast floor suggests the crossing of a chancel. The concourse ceiling is painted to represent the night sky, with signs of the Zodiac up there; far below the trains lie, socketed into their platforms, and the refreshment men with their little trays walk up and down the waiting cars, and the conductors stand at the carriage doors like retainers left from another era—coachmen superannuated, or former butlers.

All this dignity is misleading, of course. The story of New York railroads was charged with mayhem from the start, and for generations the competition between them lay viciously near the roots of New York politics. The trunk lines that ran away, one after the other, from the Bay into the interior were built in brutal rivalry. For years there was no co-operation between them, let alone any standardization of equipment: each was merely out to beat the other, whatever the cost to port or city. There was no public control, Federal, State, or civic, over their activities. Sometimes rival railroads had protégé ports, offering more favorable terms to exporters shipping via Baltimore, say, or Boston. Always the ambitions of the railway magnates were interwoven with city affairs, and so affected every aspect of the seaport's life.

The first New York railroad was the Hudson Line, which ran down Manhattan as far as Cortlandt Street, and whose tracks are still commemorated in the underpass of lower Park Avenue, below Grand Central—once a railroad tunnel. Then one by one the terminals were built on the New Jersey shore—at Bayonne, Jersey City, Hoboken, Weehawken, like so many landing stages for the hinterland. Perth Amboy was the first terminal for the Southern lines: goods from New England used to be shipped down Long Island Sound, through the East River, across the Bay and through the Kills to the New Jersey shore without touching New York soil at all. Fleets of scows and barges connected these mainland stations with Manhattan and the rest of the harbor, and there the terminals still stand, turning miles of the New Jersey bank into a mass of yards and sidings, and showing on the port maps as big blodges and streaks of red.

To a European, accustomed to State railways, it seems perfectly astonishing that even now eight separate companies own the lines that serve New York—nine until 1968, when the two patriarchs of the scene, New York Central and Pennsylvania, merged into Penn Central. Some of them look, on the map, almost nonsensical, for they were often founded in the first place as speculative ventures to feed developing rural areas, and are left now running through country with no large towns and precious little industry. No single railroad has ever crossed the United States from coast to coast: you can do it on two different systems in Canada, but in the States you always have to change trains.

Rolling stock is now interchangeable between the different American trunk lines, but it remains the property of a particular line, is painted in the company colors, and after each journey has to be returned to its owners. In the past this has entailed prodigies of calculation and maneuver, for about 1.8 million freight cars are at large on the 200,000 miles of American track. Now, since there seems no prospect of solving the problem by nationalizing the railroads, a stunningly clever automation system is doing it instead: automatic scanners respond to reflective sheets upon the freight cars, even when they are whizzing by at 60 m.p.h., and not merely make a note of the car's identity, but flash it instantaneously to a central computer in Washington, D. C. —itself automatically linked with the headquarters of subscribing railroads. At the Penn Central marshaling yard at Selkirk, New York, these techniques are carried further still, for there radar, electronic counters, photoelectric cells and closed-circuit television are all used to sort out freight cars— as the railroad's president has said, there is "an almost limitless potential of cybernetics for adoption to railroading."

To the outsider in New York, the complexity of the railway systems chiefly shows in homelier spectacles, and notably in the car floats perpetually pottering across the waters of the harbor—often apparently without means of locomotion, when the tug is hidden behind the rolling stock; for these are loaded with a wild variety of rolling stocks, all different colors, with exotic names like Wabash, Union Pacific, or Atchison, Topeka and Santa Fe—all of them, once their load is discharged, to be floated back to the mainland again, sorted out, and sent back across the continent, with inconceivable shuntings and shufflings, to their remote but expectant owners. To the port of New York this elaborate traffic has been of supreme importance. The railroad map of the United States is a convoluted affair, spindly lines radiating mishmash all over it, apparently defying the logic of geography or economics, bifurcating and multiplying dizzily, marked only by inexplicable initials and not infrequently converging upon junctions in the middle of nowhere. One railway center that does seem to make sense on this baffling chart is New York: the lines appear to make for the Bay by instinct, and there, in thickening lines of blackness as the tracks draw close to one another, one may see their pattern graphically displayed: the two big trunk lines down from the north; the suburban lines coming in from Long Island; the two which come up from Philadelphia and Washington; the three whose depots on the shores of the Hudson River are the ends of the long track from the West. They are like long extensions of the port, or cables, along which the energies and impulses of the waterfront have been transmitted, generation by generation, through the developing States.

Today, for all their cybernetic enthusiasms, the railways seem an unwieldy means of communication. They are always on the defensive. In passenger traffic they fight, here as everywhere, a losing battle against the automobile and the airlines; in the handling of freight they are threatened always by that more flexible instrument of transport, the truck. I suppose long-haul, heavy traffic will always be the prerogative of the railways, but in short-haul traffic the truck has already caught up, and it dominates the internal economy of this city. About 400,000 commercial vehicles are registered in the port district of New York; another 58,000 travel in and out of the district every day; 13,000 dump trucks handle the garbage of the metropolis alone; on a busy night 1,600 truckloads of edibles are unloaded at a single city market. In the streets of New York the truck is king: bigger than buses, louder than engines, more earth-shaking than steam hammers, clogging the cobbled back streets, eddying along the expressways—and driven still, if not so often held in rein, by the men of the Teamsters Local.

I used to love to walk northwards from Battery Point into the downtown business district, away from the fine wide prospects of the waterfront into the chasms and alleys of Wall Street, where the air seems thick with high finance, and embedded among the office blocks is that supreme totem of profit, Trinity Church—like a black gem, V. S. Pritchett thought it, but it reminds me more of one of those queer black Madonnas, pagan in origin and invested by glitter, that one finds in mystic corners of Spanish cathedrals. It is only a few hundred yards from the ferry station to the Stock Exchange, but the stroll is full of meaning.

Immediately behind the docks, in the earliest days of New York, the bankers, the merchants, the brokers, and the intelligence agents set up shop. They were ancillaries of the port. In the very same streets you may find them today, and from the balcony of the New York Stock Exchange one may look directly down Broad Street to the buildings of the waterfront. In the early days the shipowners of New York were often bankers and merchants too, and ever since the activities of the port have been inextricably enmeshed with high finance. Wall Street, the synonym of capitalism, owes its pre-eminence to the harbor, and in return it gives to this seaport a status unique to itself. Only London has so complete a range of financial services at hand; and even there the conjunction between port and city has none of the dramatic impact of New York.

To the Left there has always been something sinister about the alliance between South Street and Wall Street; on the other hand in the demonology of the Right the militant unionists of the New York waterfront have been a threat to the whole throbbing concept of the American Way, sustained as it must be by the prestige and integrity of lower Manhattan. Either way, this is the symbolic seaport of private enterprise, and how closely finance and shipping stuck together in the heyday of the tycoons you may see from the roster of benefactors at the Seamen's Church Institute: all the gilt-edged names are there, all the magnate names—a Carnegie, a Frick, a Juilliard, two Harknesses, a J. P. Morgan, a Rockefeller, two Schiffs, and three Vanderbilts. When, at midday exactly on September 16, 1920, somebody exploded a wagon of explosives in the middle of Wall Street, two prominent citizens were among those killed and injured. One was Junius Spencer Morgan, whose finger was cut when the House of Morgan was damaged. The other was Edward Sweet, founder of the most famous restaurant of the waterfront, who disappeared without trace, save only for a single finger with his ring upon it. On the walls of the House of Morgan you may still see the chips of the explosion; and at the corner of Fulton and South Street, opposite Pier 17 on the East River, Sweet's still serves the best red snapper in town.

The finance houses were originally direct adjuncts to the harbor. New York bankers, for example, financed the shipments of the "cotton triangle," and lent money to the shopkeepers of the interior to pay for their imports through the port. The first securities were traded as an accessory to foreign commerce, and the big New York wholesale industry was an offshoot of the import trade, especially in textiles. All these were extra services for the users of the port: banks to finance their enterprises, business expertise to help their commerce, wholesale outlets for their imports, insurance to keep them safe, law officers to keep them legal.

From them has arisen the whole vast commercial and financial structure that is modern New York. It has happened nowhere else, New York's combination of historical and geographical advantages being unique: probably no other seaport, for example, offers the right geological foundation for such a complex of skyscrapers as Manhattan's—themselves, with their tremendous concentration of people and services, a major business convenience. New York is so unchallenged a center of American business that of the 500 biggest American corporations, 139 have their head offices in this city. If speed and innovation are the qualities required, New York more than anywhere else on earth is qualified to help: just as in the sailing ship days, if you needed a fast packet or a captain who knew the route, South Street was your place.

So New York casts a kind of spell across its hinterland, partly attributable to the magic of its name, partly to its expertise. The most spectacular symptom of this ascendancy is the New York Stock Exchange, which was founded in 1792 around the corner from Trinity Church, and now occupies a big neo-Classical structure which would do well as a saluting base for a victory parade of brokers, if ever Wall Street felt that the triumph of it philosophies was complete.

Inside, its appeal is less stately. It looks like a kind of madhouse. The Exchange does not pretend to exclusivity. Overwhelmingly male though it is, it has none of the reserved pride of a club. It aims to draw its funds from as wide a social origin as possible, and it is only too anxious to display itself to visitors. Girls in uniform greet you when you cross those resplendent portals, and give you shiny explanatory pamphlets, and show you exhibits in glass cases, and then usher you, talking educationally as they go, into the public gallery.

Below you a multitude of men *twitches*. There must be a couple of thousand of males down there, and scarcely one of them is still. They are all walking about, or flipping note-books up and down, or picking up telephones, or scribbling in pads, or searching for somebody else, or taking papers out of dockets, or waving at friends, or going out, or coming in again, or looking up at the girls in the gallery, or simply crossing and recrossing their legs as they sit nervously medi-tating on stools beside their desks. There never was such a restless scene. Strips of illuminated numerals run along the walls, like the news flashes in Times Square. A big illuminated clock shifts numerals every minute. Two vast boards are covered with numbered plates, which keep flipping testily up and down with metallic clickings, telling brokers beneath when they are wanted at their booths. Millions of pieces of paper are scrunched and shuffled around the floor.

The Stock Exchange is an intelligence agency not merely for New York, but for the whole United States, and for the world. Its fluctuations both reflect and influence the state of the nations. Its members come from 350 American cities, and most of them are in immediate teletype communication with their home offices. The clearing of information is an original function of New York, deriving directly from the port. The packet boats first made this place the chief news center of the United States: the New York newspapers had their own sloops and schooners to meet the incoming ships from Europe, racing each other out to Sandy Hook, often before the pilot boats themselves, to be first with the dis-patches from London and the Continent. Later the incoming ships released carrier pigeons, which took the news to a tele-graph station at Sandy Hook. It was to New York, too, that the pony couriers, and later the stagecoaches, labored with their mails and dispatches across the Appalachians: from this port the coastal ships and packets could distribute the news from the interior across the world.

This primacy has never been lost. New York is the world's most active communications center. It might be said that television as a culture, or at least a public obsession, was born in this port; the chief American radio and television networks all have their headquarters there. So do the news agencies and the great advertising firms, and the only two daily papers that might claim to be national journals are the *New York Times* and the *Wall Street Journal.* One can only be saddened by the decline of the New York daily press: the homesick journalists one so often meets, exiled to Government or public relations; the grand old premises, of *World Telegram* or *Herald Tribune,* now debased to more prosaic functions; the traces of forgotten papers, *Mirrors* and *Banners* and *Telegraphs,* one comes across in public libraries and historical memoirs. I have to admit, all the same, that in New York today the sense of immediate contact with the world's happenings could hardly be more urgent, and sometimes I used to stand at night beneath the Times Square news strip and soak the sensation pleasurably in: above my head the bulletin whirred round and round in neon letters, around the corner the *Times* was going to press, and everywhere I fancied the hum of the nightly news.

And then, sometimes, I would be seized with a kind of revelation, and as I walked away through the busy streets I would feel the night active with the traffic of intelligence. Then it would seem to me that the New Yorkers, who appear for the most part a private kind of people, walking withdrawn along the sidewalks deep in their anxieties—then the New Yorkers would suddenly seem linked secretly by their own arcane network of communications, on wave lengths all their own. Up and down the cliff faces of the apartment houses I would see the flicker of the television sets, each a symbol of this collusion, and down the hotel corridors the fruity television voices issuing from behind each door sounded like the instructions of conspirators to a disciplined community.

At such a moment all the movements and innuendoes of New York seem figuratively intensified. The lights shine balefully, high on the summit of the Empire State. The radar scanners ominously swirl. As a police car prowls by one can hear the distorted voice of some dispatcher far away, and at Grand Central the closed-circuit television screens flicker their dim regulations to the masses. The island then is full of noises. I think of the mass of encoded messages pouring in, night and day, to the tall shining palace of the United Nations; of the frenzied telex worrying away the Wall Street hours; of the ships reporting to New York, as they pass Nantucket Point and swing down east for Sandy Hook, and the airliners circling in their fretful stacks above Long Island; of all the telephoning ladies of New York, yackety-yak through the evening, and the radio taxis, and the tugs talking their liners in, and the myriad computers of the city, and all the beams reaching out of New York like rays from a great fire—to ships in the most distant seas, to capitals across the world, or to the spinning satellites beyond the sky.

All this, I used to think when I recovered from my purple passages, out of that harbor—which, when the first stones were laid of my house in Wales, was no more than a patch of clear water, frequented only by feathered primitives, and seen by no more than a handful of literate men! But in New York, I discovered, when one has got into a properly maritime frame of mind, things fall into a different pattern. When I walked from the Battery to Trinity Church now I could see the influence of the waterfront permeating the business district; then, higher up the island, came the garment quarter, a depository of foreign trade: and finally, even in midtown Manhattan, where not so long before I had noticed only the Members Only signs, or the Exclusive to Us, now I saw all about me evidences of the port.

Here are the airline offices, and the travel agencies, and the cruise advertisements—the Bacchus Cruise, the Valentine Cruise, the Grand Slam Cruise, the Wonderful World of the Caribbean. Here is the Curaçao Information Center, and the Norwegian Consulate. Even the glorious museums and art galleries of Manhattan are an aspect of portage: for if, as the statistics say, the principal goods handled by the port of New York are machinery, chemicals, textiles, vehicles, steel products, sugar, bananas, coffee, newsprint, vegetable oils, grain, ore, and petroleum—if these are the things that appear on the lading bills, many less tangible commodities are imported and exported too. Ideas of every kind pour in and out of New York—refined in the city, often enough, like the petroleum, adapted or given new energy, and shipped out east and west. Manhattan is one of the great art exchanges of the world, one of the great theater cities, one of the great fashion centers. Through New York all the American philosophies, from the Jeffersonian via the revivalist to the hippy, have been shipped to other countries; through New York all the inventions of Europe, French hairdos or English plays or Italian vermouth or German cars, are disseminated throughout the United States.

The port made it. Because of the port the United Nations has its palace on the East River; and the splendors and the torments of New York, which have made this place the epitome of Western civilization, spring from the waterfront. Having traced, in my own passage through the port, the movements of freight and of history into the harbor, across the city, and out into the hinterland, now I began to contemplate the implications of portage to this city, and to observe how many scars, splashes of color, and sad scraps of debris are left behind by its momentum.

Three

ALLEGORICAL

Chapter 12

DEPOSITS

At first I thought of New York's allegories simply as deposits. A geological metaphor was proper, it seemed, because New York itself is built of layers, or sediments. Physically the original islets, flats, and sandbanks of the archipelago have been artificially transformed. The whole outer rim of Manhattan is man-made, and is still periodically extended—the very cobblestones mostly came here as ballast from Europe. In 1660, as we may see from the Castello Plan of New Amsterdam, Fort Amsterdam, on the site of the present Custom House, was at the water's edge, and only a single block of houses and gardens separated Broadway from the Hudson—today there are four blocks and an expressway. On the other side of Manhattan Pearl Street was the waterfront then; in successive generations Water Street was added, then Front Street, and finally South Street. When Trinity Church was built its graveyard ran to the water's edge, now out of sight from the tombstones, and the whole of the North River waterfront, with all its passenger piers, was created by engineers. In the 1830s there was an official plan to build an enormous breakwater in the middle of the Hudson, as long as Manhattan itself, 200 feet wide and honeycombed with storage cellars. In the 1820s two hoaxers had gone further still. They announced that the southern end of Manhattan, then still joined to the Bronx by a spit across the Harlem River, was sinking under the weight of its buildings and they proposed to saw it off and turn it round the other way, using 20 saws 100 feet long, and 24 oars 250 feet long, each to be manned by 100 oarsmen. Three hundred men applied to work upon this scheme—they were told they would get triple pay if they could hold their breath long enough to do the underwater sawing—but though a drum and fife band turned up on contract day to lead the labor force to work, the engineers were nowhere to be found.

In the reclaimed areas of New York the water level is only five feet below street level, and engineers erecting skyscrapers near the waterfront today must first sink waterproof caissons beneath ground level, as though they are building a river bridge. Even so, more land is reclaimed from the Bay each year. Te get sand fill for Newark Airport and the new docks at Port Elizabeth, four tugs with barges worked day and night for three years, sucking up sand off Sandy Hook. A favorite raw material nowadays is refuse: like Venice, much of New York is built upon garbage.

Metaphysically too New York is artificially layered. To me it still feels consciously created—not like the European capitals, which seem merely to have grown, like old trees of the forests, but deliberately unloaded there upon the foreshore, and staked about, and added to, and restarted, and given calculated infusions of fresh concrete, and then rejigged again, and extended and adapted year by year. V. S. Pritchett makes the daring point that all in all not very much has happened in New York, and it is true that there is something throwaway or disposable to the genius of the place. It does not appear to be an end in itself: it is only the layered residue of energies rushing through, as a torrent leaves its grooves and strange patterns upon the walls of a gorge. New York has little respect for permanence. Its skyscrapers are usually knocked down again after forty or fifty years, and in a city notorious for the accumulation of wealth, most New Yorkers I know really do not set much store upon possessions.

I sat one day with a New York tycoon whose new skyscraper building was even then arising, across the street from the old office in which we sat. I found this a stirring experience. His mother, still living, he told me, had arrived almost penniless in New York sixty years before, from Eastern Europe—with a label hung around her neck, proclaiming her skills to the employers who waited upon the docks in those days, looking for likely labor. His rise to fame and fortune had a heroic quality to it that I much admired, and I thought it a fine thing to look out of the window that day and see his own great tower arising proudly there. It was a shame, I remarked, that by the time the next generation of his family grew up, it would probably be demolished.

But he was not in the least depressed by the thought. To him New York was essentially an *abrupt* city, where things happened with a rush, and did not last long. He shared the geological view—the conception of this city as a groove in history, its buildings like boulders left behind, its boulevards like fossil scars. "It takes a great people," was all he said, "to put up such buildings—and pull them down again."

So mercurial is the nature of New York that the city has never set. "A European city," Lord Bryce called it half a century ago, "but of no particular country." Today one could never mistake it for anywhere in Europe, hard though many European capitals try to copy it, but still it has never been altogether Americanized. "Ah, but New York is not America," Americans always tell the foreigner, and it is true that New York, more than most comparable cities in other

countries, stands separate from the generality. London and
Paris are fair microcosms of their States. New York is not.
The standard veneer of the Americans has never quite lac-
quered New York, and in a nation dedicated to ideals of
sameness, standardization, togetherness, egality, this port remains vividly and sometimes parlously different.

In 1643 a French traveler recorded that 18 languages were
spoken in New York. Today there are newspapers published
in at least 20, the public libraries lend books in 30, and there
are 75 ethnic groups large enough to have organizations of
their own. To this day nearly half the people of New York
are of foreign birth or parentage, and if anything, I think,
they resist assimilation more firmly than their fathers did.
The Negroes and Puerto Ricans are certainly more conscious
of their own heritages, but even the Greeks and Italians, in
the past the most anxious to salute the flag, take the oath, or
express All-American sentiments, now seem prouder of their
separate origins. Exotic given names appear more frequently
in the school rosters, and it is no longer only Daughters of
the American Revolution who make pilgrimages to their
ancestral homes, or hang framed family trees where their
neighbors can see them.

Of course there are millions of New Yorkers who appear
to be simply Americans: all the Anglo-Saxons, for instance,
many of the Jews, and vast numbers of Italians, Germans,
Irishmen, and Scandinavians. "Where did your people origi-
nate?" I once asked an eminent executive of the Port Authority. "Brooklyn," he haughtily replied. But in many parts
of the city there are ethnic quarters as clearly defined, and
often as prickly, as any Armenian enclave of medieval Europe.
It is as though their particular communities, Greeks or
Ukrainians or Spaniards, have disembarked from Ellis Island,
decamped to their respective quarters of the city, and stayed

there ever since—except that sometimes whole communities
have migrated within New York, and moved their beer halls
or their jazz clubs, their pizza bars or their skittle alleys uptown or across a river.

A world of sadness, courage, and uncertainty is reflected
in this patchwork New York. Immigration sounds a noble
process, conveyed in soulful verse upon a plinth, but it was
not always so inspiring in the event. Many immigrants came
to New York only because ships with space were sailing
there: once landed at Battery Point they had neither money,
nor initiative, nor incentive to go any further. Others,
especially poor Italians, were encouraged over in their hundreds of thousands to provide cheap labor for expanding
industries—and were sometimes met at the waterfront by
native-born New Yorkers savagely determined to keep their
own jobs. Race feeling has always run high on the New York
waterfront—Irish versus southern Italians, blacks versus
whites—and no doubt, as the poor immigrants moved into
their tenements away from the harbor, these prejudices infected the rest of the city too.

So there is pathos to the ethnic variety of this seaport: these
were people, I presently began to feel, bunched together for
comfort in the most thrusting, heartless, and demanding environment on earth. It has long been a travel writer's cliché,
of course, that there are more Irish in New York than in
Dublin, more Italians than in Naples, more Jews than in Tel
Aviv. More interesting to me were the lesser minorities, only
a few thousand strong, who nevertheless honor their own
mores, speak their own tongues, and often occupy their own
quarters of town. There are the Albanians, who live on the
lower East Side, and the Armenians on Washington Heights,
and the Bulgarians with their own cathedral on 101st Street,
and the Czechs with their twice-weekly *New Yorke Listy,*

and the Finns of Brooklyn, and the old French neighborhood around Ninth Avenue in the 50s, and the Greeks with their two daily papers, and the Japanese who celebrate the Festival of O-bon with outdoor dances around 110th Street, and the Norwegians who have their own Independence Day parade on May 17th in Brooklyn, and the Portuguese in Greenwich Village, and the Rumanians with their National Committee on West 57th Street, and the Turkish Cypriots in the East Bronx, and the Arabic-speaking Jews, and the Koreans who have their own Methodist Church, and the Dutch, the original New Yorkers, proudly represented on East 78th Street by the Society of Daughters of Holland Dames. The most overwhelming immigrants are the Puerto Ricans, 800,-000 of them since the Second World War, whose presence has vastly altered the atmosphere of Manhattan, and made Spanish virtually an official language. The most imperturbable are probably the Bretons, who mostly live in the 60s around First Avenue, who dominate the waiters' profession, who bring up their children with French peasant strictness, and who nearly all intend to go home to Brittany again, when they have made enough money.

Think of the passions, inherited and acquired, which must animate these peoples, many of them old enemies, deposited now side by side amidst the cross fire of black-white hostility! I used to imagine them like so many national brigades, each with its formation signs and old battle honors, landing at the bridgehead of the Battery and advancing northwards in fragile alliance into Manhattan. Just the register of their religions sounds inflammatory, not to speak of their historical prejudices, their peculiarities of national habit, and those plain unreasoning dislikes that plague most of us in one context or another. Thomas Dongan, an Irish Catholic Governor of British New York, reported ironically in the 1680s that the port supported chaplains of the Church of England,

Dutch Calvinist, French Calvinist, and Dutch Lutheran faiths, besides "ranting Quakers; preachers men, and women especially; singing Quakers; anti-Sabbatarians; some Baptists, some independents, some Jews, in short, of all sorts of opinions there are some, and the most part of none at all."

Down the years the sects have erected their particular shrines and tabernacles all over New York. On Fort Washington Avenue St. Frances Xavier Cabrini, the first American citizen to be canonized, lies in a crystal coffin in her shrine within the Mother Cabrini High School. On Lexington and 76th is the Church of St. Jean-Baptiste, presented to the French-Canadians of New York by Thomas Ryan, who performed a public service of more equivocal effect by financing the first New York subway. On Second Avenue at 15th Street is St. Mary's, a church of the Byzantine-Jacobite rite, whose liturgical language is Old Slavonic. The handsome old Sea and Land Church, on Henry Street, was originally Dutch Reformed and is now the home of the First Chinese Presbyterian Church. Another well-known Chinese church is the True Light Church of the Missouri Synod; Huguenots worship in French at L'Eglise du St. Esprit, on East 60th Street; Holy Trinity Church on East 74th Street is the seat of the Greek Orthodox Archbishop of North and South America. There are two Buddhist temples in New York, and two orthodox mosques, besides the mosque of the Black Muslims; and in the Negro quarter of Harlem sects and subsects proliferate so dizzily, above tobacconists' shops or with grandiloquent choirs in social clubs, that a walk through the region on a Sunday morning is a discordant concert of hymns, sacred declamations, and cries of ecstasy.

Nor need you go into what New Yorkers call "the neighborhoods" to sense the foreignness of New York. I am not thinking of the innumerable foreign restaurants and cafés which offer you raw fish or retsina in the center of Manhattan; I am thinking in particular of the great Gothic cathedral of St. Patrick's, based upon the plans of Cologne and Rheims Cathedrals, with its twin spires and its seventy stained-glass windows and the line of its Archbishops buried in the crypt. This, the principal church of the Roman Catholic faith in the most sophisticated city in the world, stands in the most opulent site in Manhattan, on Fifth Avenue at 50th Street, between Saks and Best's, and opposite Rockefeller Center. Any time of day, and during much of the night, its nave is full of worshipers; and half of them might have come direct from hill villages of Italy or Connemara crofts—their faces weathered still by the hardships of the peasant life, their eyes alight with simpler convictions than Manhattan is commonly supposed to command. I often went in there, not to worship but to look at the worshipers; and it gave me an odd feeling of time truncated to emerge from their earthy presence into the blaze of Fifth Avenue.

The ethnic slabs are piled against each other most strikingly in the lower East Side of Manhattan, perhaps the most extraordinary urban district anywhere in the world. Here the deposits of the harbor are displayed almost like a parable. It is a poor area, running northward from the downtown financial district to the east side of Greenwich Village, traditionally the artists' quarter of New York. Through the drab geometrical streets of this area (new public housing projects rising blankly above the tenements) successive waves of immigrants, moving up from the wharves, have settled and moved on: poor English, Scots, and Welsh first; then the Continental immigrants, Germans, Hungarians, Italians, with Irish and Jews of many nationalities; Chinese, too, in the middle of the nineteenth century, and in our own times Negroes and Puerto Ricans by the thousand, with a late layer of salt, spice, and smut provided by the intelligentsia of the New

Lower East Side

In the bus terminal

Rush hour, Manhattan

Rush hour, Lincoln Tunnel

Rush hour, John F. Kennedy International Airport

Left—whose frailer acolytes, escaping from the proprieties of suburban and provincial life, found it easy to disappear into this old warren, shack up in a loft or a basement, and let the rest of the world go by.

This uneasy genesis has left the lower East Side in an overwrought but enthralling condition. Such sights to see! Such faces, numb or preternaturally vivacious, to stare back as you pass! We leave the waterfront behind us, pass between the banks and the brokers, and find ourselves almost at once in Chinatown. Here for a start is a community that has, it appears, only reluctantly accepted the American Way. The Chinese have been in their few streets of the lower East Side for more than a century, but the tinsel glitter of their culture shines there still, on drab façade above crowded sidewalk, defying the credit cards of the restaurants and the svelte modernity of the real-estate offices—expressed in the snails, herbs, and dried ducks of the grocery stores, the lines of Chinese children waiting to view their own past in the Chinese Museum, the six Chinese newspapers and the Chinese Opera, the clink of the Chinese language all about, and the verveless withdrawal of the Chinese faces in the street, which gives these people even now the look of exiles.

Up now along the Bowery, into the tumbled areas around Delancey Street where successive waves of immigration have left their mark. Here was once the ghetto of New York, where heavily bearded Jews were pictured in old daguerreotypes huddled over intricate crafts, or pumping water out of street pumps, looking up sidelong at the camera with sharp ambitious eyes. They came from every country of Eastern Europe, and they made this a metropolis of the Jewish culture. The Jews have gone up in the world since then, have handsomely fulfilled the promise of the daguerreotypes, and are scattered throughout New York, many of them rich or famous; but there are still survivors on the lower East Side to remind us of that vanished New York era, when the families who inhabited these tenements were still locked in their own Hebrew culture, timidly aloof to the world outside. Their quicksilver faces still look back at us through the windows of the diamond market in the Bowery, Cyclopean with an eyeglass as a stone is held to the light, or carefully focused through thick-lensed spectacles upon the approaching customer; and here a Yiddish theater survives, and there in Orchard Street, like a Jerusalem bazaar, the secondhand clothes dealers, stall by stall beneath the high tenements, still call out their bargains winningly.

Mulberry Street and the last of Little Italy: the Italian ladies in the bakers' shops, their stockings rolled above the knee, showing their fine thighs unashamed as they sit awaiting their loaves: instant laughter, and Chianti bottles, and occasionally an honest trattoria, where the tablecloths are check, Mama is in the kitchen, and *Cue* Magazine has not yet stuck its accolade upon the window. Here all the things that Italians like are bought and sold in noisy little shops. Old people still talk to you in the peculiar Italian-English that elsewhere seems to survive only in period films and old-fashioned comedy acts, and everywhere we seem to see those very same people, those fine old mustachioed men and primped little girls, whom we encountered when we met the *Raffaello* at the pier.

Up to the Essex Street market, and here the full tide of immigration swirls about us, as foreign as ever it was. Across the way Bernstein's Restaurant claims convincingly to be the original home of Kosher Chinese Food, and inside the big market, I used to feel, nowhere on earth could feel more alien to a Briton. Peculiar gourds and unappetizing offals are sold there, Negroes, Jews, Chinese, and Puerto Ricans swirl all around, there are black people talking Spanish and Greeks eating Cuban sandwiches. The streets outside are dismal with all the run-down melancholy of a ghetto, flies swarming on the corner garbage heaps, women in curlers gazing vacantly out of high windows as they do their washing, wizened little pots of plants forlorn on dirty window sills. Here is all the ugliness of immigration. There are worn-out people everywhere, bow-legged, embittered, clamoring through these unlovely *suks* like impoverished Orientals. I used to watch them wonderingly, comparing the splendor and agony of their different heritages with my own easy origins: my people constant in their happy islands since the Druids, theirs swept hither and thither across the continents, persecuted or triumphant, sometimes masters, sometimes serfs, until at last the greatest tide of all flooded them into this tumultuous seaport of the West.

North again now, picking our way through the down-and-outs snoring on the Bowery sidewalks, past the throaty sound of chanting from a basement synagogue, while the big silver buses sweep past in incongruous grandeur, and up towards Tompkins Square. Here intermingled with the first boutiques and avant-garde cafés are the dark shops of the Ukrainians, where brown wrinkled old ladies wear babushka scarves over their heads, and men in brown hats speak no English. Here are the onion domes of the Ukrainian Catholic Church, and sometimes one hears a snatch of Slav invective from the stairs of a brownstone house. There are Poles about, too, and Russians, and a few Germans, and crowding down the side streets, bursting from tenements, gay and volatile and dangerous, multitudes of Puerto Ricans.

And so we saunter into Tompkins Square, the Place de la Concorde or perhaps more appropriately the Trafalgar Square of the lower East Side. Here the melting pot bubbles at its hottest but least effectual, and half a dozen cultures glare at

each other across the scuffled garden. It is not a beautiful
plaza. Litter blows across it, its surrounding houses are peeling
and unpainted, the sauntering crowds are either very poor or
preposterously exhibitionist. But a hint of danger gives an
excitement to Tompkins Square, and alleviates its squalor.

In the corner café the drop-outs of society lie tumbled
in hairy and emaciated heaps, holding guitars, like drugged
travelers at an Indian railroad station. Across the way a
crowd of young Puerto Ricans is shrilly disputing a point
of economics with a grocer, all black eyes and gesticula-
tions, with a dubious cop poised on the sidewalk behind,
night stick in hand. Half a dozen rangy Negro youths come
patrolling across the gardens, like a commando on the move,
eyes alert, long lean fingers hanging by the thumbs from
trouser pockets, all alive with animal grace and force. Pottering through it all are homely old Europeans with shopping
bags, and a few dazed tourists with cameras and street plans,
and pairs of wide-eyed girls from more conventional parts
of town, living it up with uncomprehending little faces and
unnecessary cigarettes ("That's what I like to see," said one
such visitor to another in my hearing, apparently referring
to a kind of amulet-strung Caliban shambling by in a thick-
ened smock, "dressed like that, real *sharp*").

Scarcely a standard, orthodox, middle-class, native-born
American of capitalist philosophy lives in these parts. These
are the deposits uncongealed, and evidently uncongealable.
From upstairs windows esoteric faces occasionally look out,
of indeterminate age, sex, race, or intention, shrouded in
black hair, in pajamas or dungarees or raincoats—people who
seem to occupy no particular place in the world, cherish no
definable loyalties, demand no privileges, but have simply
been washed up on this crowded foreshore by the tide of the
great port, like flotsam off the sea.

But often the deposits do harden, into marvelous forms. All the museums, galleries, libraries, and concert halls of New York have solidified out of the same tide, and there are many men of great gifts who have seized out of all this complexity the materials of a splendid culture. Let me introduce you to two of them, anonymously: one a poet, one a millionaire.

The poet lives, as it happens, a few hundred yards from Tompkins Square, in a street that is almost grotesquely avant-garde on the surface, but is given a solider base by the presence of Ukrainian and Polish families, entrenched among the pads and boutiques like badgers in a fun fair. It reminds me sometimes of Montmartre and sometimes of London's Chelsea, but is tinged orientally, too, with odors of incense and suggestions of guru and hashish. The place is divided between old immigrants and new, coloreds and whites, beer drinkers and drug addicts, heteros and homos, the Catholic and the Zen, the schmaltzy and the psychedelic.

Halfway up the right-hand side of the street, as you walk away from Tompkins Square, you will see the shabby bow-windowed office of a law firm, its name printed in old gold lettering upon black-painted glass. An uncarpeted flight of stairs passes their door on the ground floor, turns one flight up, and gives access to an apartment; and there ensconced among books and pictures lives, for a large part of every year, one of the two or three most celebrated poets of the twentieth century.

He lives very simply up there. He cooks for himself, and makes coffee for his visitors. His surroundings are not exactly shabby, but are noticeably well worn. Sofas have deep declivities in their seats. Books cover every snatch of available wall, and through the window the poet may look out to the seething complexity of the street below. Everything about this apartment is real. Nothing is there for effect. Its occupant could live and work anywhere he pleased in the world, and spends part of each year, indeed, on the continent of Europe, and part at one of the ancient English universities; but for the urban part of his life, the part perhaps that is rechargeable, like a battery plugged into a dynamo, he chooses to come to this frenzied and gaudy corner of the seaport. He might find a better apartment somewhere else, but in no other city could he feel that surge, eddy, and backwash outside his window.

The poet is there by choice. The millionaire is a New Yorker by birth. He is the end product, the pebble worn smooth and symmetrical until it looks like some exquisite artifact of the sea. I wrote to this rich man one day, explaining my purpose, admitting that I knew few New Yorkers in his league, and asking if I might come and look at the way he lived, for literary purposes. By all means, his secretary promptly replied, her eyebrows slightly raised over the telephone, and so one evening I took a cab to his house, and knocked on the door.

It opened, and there in the bright lights lay the ultimate commodity of this port: highly cultivated wealth. It was a house that could only exist in New York. At first I thought it might as well be in London, but presently I realized there were differences in kind. My host and hostess behaved more or less as any comparable European couple might behave, when entertaining a guest not merely totally unknown to them, but nosy by definition; but the great difference was that these people were not in any way nostalgic. They were citizens of a city of change, and were not concerned with their own past. They were anything but *nouveaux-riches,* having been born into a Harvard-and-Tiffany milieu that was several generations old, but still they seemed to have started from scratch.

No lugubrious ancestral portraits looked down from those

walls: instead, mouth-watering French Impressionists hung there, misty Monets above the sofa table, a Bonnard I would give my left arm for. Lovely objects were everywhere, hall to landing, down to eighteenth-century Chinese wallpaper, made for the English market but never before unrolled, in which no glorious little bird was ever once repeated. At first I distrusted my host's infatuation for these things, having a prejudice against connoisseurs anyway, and detesting the degradation of art into an investment, but presently I realized that he really loved his possessions. He showed them to me with true affection, and told me that he often moved his pictures around the room, to enjoy the variation of light and setting. They were mostly very peaceful scenes: a change from the office, he said.

Yet even he, a man of power as well as taste, commanding everything that money can buy—even he seemed restless and impatient: not socially, for he was kindness itself, but temperamentally. The whole luxurious establishment seemed to me somehow disposable: the manservant, the housekeeper, the masterpieces on the walls, the carpets from the East, the gorgeous lamps and calf-bound library, the great silver tray of decanters and silver-topped siphons, the bronze picked up from an unknown but infinitely promising young sculptor during a recent visit to West Africa—none of it seemed designed to last. It was as though my millionaire might decide one day to rip it all up and start again. As he saw me off at the door two things happened. An alarm buzzer sounded, announcing that the eldest son of the house had got stuck in the private elevator; and the millionaire's wife called through the drawing-room door to say that the White House was on the telephone. "Excuse me," he said in his flat velvet voice, shaking hands on the doorstep. "I have one or two things to attend to. Thanks for coming."

I picked up a cab on Fifth Avenue that night, and as we drove home through the night I told the driver of my visits to the poet and the plutocrat. "What a combination!" was his response. "Both living on immoral earnings! What kind of a book are you writing, anyway? Pornography?"

Chapter 13

IMPLICATIONS

For of course New York, founded upon the ambitions and rivalries of the sea, is a place of conflict. Every city has its antagonisms, but in New York they show more, and hurt more, because of the vital energy of the place—that insatiable appetite for movement which is itself revolutionary by nature. To many of New York's visitors the implications of the city are universal: the dream going sour, the brotherhood of man denied hour by hour in rudeness, dishonesty, suspicion, and violence. Others believe that the historic point of New York today, the root of its contemporary character, is the twentieth-century racial conflict, heightened in this city (like everything else) by the force of the environment. For myself, I came to feel that if we must take New York as the archetype of our Western, urban civilization, it is not because human nature is nastier than we supposed, nor because of transient antagonisms of color, but because here the pace of material progress is set: the progress of perpetual change, which stimulates the spirit too far, cuts us off from the springs of certainty, and leaves us spinning nervously and testily from unnecessary challenge to trumped-up response. Mr. Tobin's New York, the New York of dazzling technical enterprise, is the most exciting place in the world, as I suspect it has been since the middle of the nineteenth century. Talking sometimes with its representatives, communications men or aviation experts, I used to feel that the present was already fading, and we had actually entered the future. It seemed to me that there was nothing this astonishing people could not achieve, and no power that was not within their grasp.

Yet even more potent than the promise of New York, I thought, was its clash: from the rude retort in the supermarket to the savagery of the neighborhoods, the fear that haunts the city parks at nighttime, the young men senselessly throwing their stones at the engines, when the fire brigade answers a call.

New York knows little of war. The last shot fired here in military anger was fired in the War of 1812, by warships off the Bay. The last battle fought on the soil of the city was the battle of Harlem Heights in 1776, when Washington drove the British off the site of 119th Street, and proved it could be done. There was plenty of fighting here in the pioneering days, when the Dutch, the British, and the Indians engaged in a succession of campaigns and massacres; in modern times this city of commerce has fought its battles at a distance, or won its wars by prevention.

So seductive a prize has always been heavily defended. In sailing-ship days the harbor was thought to be impregnable, so elaborate were its fortifications. There were batteries of guns on both sides of the Narrows, and supporting batteries on Governors Island, Bedloe's Island, Ellis Island, and the foot of Manhattan—Battery Point. Some two hundred yards off the foot of Hubert Street, in lower Manhattan, a mid-river fort of red sandstone commanded the entrance to the Hudson; Fort Williams on Governors Island covered the East River. All these batteries were carefully enfiladed, and traces of many can still be seen: the fine old forts of Wadsworth and Hamilton still salute each other across the Narrows, one at each end of the Verrazano Bridge; Governors Island still bristles with antique defiance, Castle Williams in enfilade with Castle Clinton on the Battery, South Battery commanding the Buttermilk Channel (though it is an officers' club now, and faces the water with nothing more lethal in hand than a whisky sour).

In both world wars steel antisubmarine nets were placed across the Narrows, and today Castles Clinton and Williams, Forts Hamilton and Wadsworth, are reinforced by batteries out of sight: missile batteries dispersed around the perimeter of the city, fighter squadrons on Long Island and in New Jersey. In the Second World War the military jurisdiction of the army headquarters on Governors Island covered forty States, besides American forces in Greenland, Iceland, Bermuda, and Newfoundland. Now I am told the defense headquarters for this part of the United States is somewhere in southern New Jersey; but I did not inquire further, and saw hardly a sign of warlike preparation throughout my passage through New York—a warship or two, gray two-funneled troopships moored at Bayonne, faded Civil Defense instructions in public places, the printed information that if ever there were a nuclear attack on the port, the twenty-four municipal ferryboats, snatched from the Staten Island run, would be used to carry citizens across the water to safety.

The harbor has often been threatened. In 1813 British cruisers lay off Sandy Hook for weeks at a time, and foreign goods had to be smuggled into New Jersey and taken overland to New York. During the Civil War the captain of the Confederate cruiser *Tallahassee* cherished a grand design to steal through the Narrows at night, sink the shipping in the harbor and the East River, beat up the Brooklyn Navy Yard, and escape *via* Hell Gate and the Sound; he tried to induce captured Sandy Hook pilots to guide him into the Bay, but they declined and the plan was unfortunately abandoned—

for one can hardly imagine a more dashing or enjoyable exploit. In the First World War German saboteurs from the liner *Friedrich der Grosse*, immobilized in New York harbor before America's entry into the war, blew up several ships' cargoes bound for Allied countries. In the Second World War German submarines often prowled off-shore, sometimes entering the Sound, and even dropping an inept selection of agents on the Long Island shore: scores of New York yachtsmen joined the Coast Guard Temporary Reserve, and took their sloops and schooners—*Sea Gypsy*, *Kidnaper*, *Sunbeam*—gamely out to sea in search of them.

Much more often, though, New York has sent its ships and men to fight elsewhere. In the War of 1812 shipbuilders from the port went to work on Lake Erie, and it was the ships they built up there that kept the Royal Navy at bay on the Great Lakes, and perhaps prevented a British invasion from the north. The most famous was Noah Brown, master shipbuilder, about whom just a century later the poet W. R. Rose wrote a pair of stirring stanzas in the Cleveland *Plain Dealer*:

> *Times were troubled, they all agree,*
> *Foes were scourging the inland sea,*
> *Rumors, panics and daily scares*
> *Steeped the patriot soul in cares;*
> *Fear was rampant and hope was down—*
> *Then they rallied and sent for Brown.*
>
> *This is the message the rider bore:*
> *"Boats are needed on Erie's shore!"*
> *What did the builder do or say?*
> *Saddled his nag and rode away;*
> *Leaping, fording to Erie town—*
> *"How many boats?" quoth Noah Brown.*

A hundred and thirty years later hundreds of shipbuilders from the Brooklyn Navy Yard saddled their nags just as readily and leaped away to Pearl Harbor, to repair ships damaged by the Japanese attack. For a century and half their yard, whose old gray installations still stand beside the East River, built ships for the American Navy. The meticulously cut granite blocks of its Dry Dock Number 1, completed in 1851, still look as good as new, and nearby stand six later docks which have handled ships as varied as the *Monitor,* fitted out in the yard in 1862, and the battleship *Missouri,* launched there in 1944. It seemed so extraordinary to me that this immense warship should be constructed in so public a place in the middle of a world war that I looked up the launching in the file of the *New York Times,* half expecting it to have been blacked out by censorship. Far from it. New York is the very fountain of publicity, and not even a world war could stifle the port's sense of occasion. "World's Greatest Warship Is Launched in Brooklyn," said the headline; and far from being shrouded in secrecy, I gathered, the launching had been celebrated as bravely as any passenger liner's maiden voyage, in the flamboyant days of peace. At least twenty thousand spectators crowded both banks of the East River, and tugs and ships all over the port blew their whistles as the ship slid down the way—slicked, the Navy tells me, with a mixture of mush and banana skins, though the *Times* called it "special greases." Miss Margaret Truman christened the battleship with a bottle of champagne made from Missouri grapes—as good a use, perhaps, as could be made of it. Senator Truman of Missouri made a speech, and a message from Admiral Halsey expressed the view that ships like the *Missouri* would "prove the wallop to flatten Tojo and his crew." In this he was prophetic, for it was upon the deck of the *Missouri,* within two years, that Tojo and his crew surrendered once and for all to the power of the United States.

Many another proud ship has sailed to battle from this harbor, or returned here as a haven from the wars. A great New York occasion was the return of the victorious American fleet from the Spanish-American War, in 1898. Flags aflutter, their rails lined by sailors in spanking tropical white, five battleships and two cruisers steamed slowly through the Bay, attended by four hundred tugs, schooners, launches, and steamboats. Up the Hudson they sailed, cheered by vast crowds upon the shore, and dropping anchor off Grant's Tomb they celebrated the victory of Santiago Bay with a twenty-one-gun salute from each ship—the puffs of white smoke drifting over the Palisades, the cheers echoing away, I dare say, to the immigrant tenements downtown, where Jews recently arrived from the ghettoes of Europe must have wondered where the war had been this time.

The great convoys that assembled here in both world wars must have been a sight to see, gray and storm-beaten as they gathered their strength for the dangerous haul to Europe. The maiden arrival of the *Queen Elizabeth*, too, for she sailed into New York in 1940 unannounced—uncompleted from her shipyard on the Clyde, painted a gloomy gray, the biggest liner ever built suddenly arrived at the Ambrose Light early on a March morning, to be greeted only by three astonished blasts of a hooter from the sludge boat *Coney Island*. Many a New York tug has sailed from this harbor to warlike adventures in distant seas: Admiral Moran, of the tug company, organized the greatest of all towing operations when he delivered two complete Mulberry Harbors, towed by two hundred tugs, upon the coast of France for the Normandy invasions.

Marvelous scenes of triumph and relief have been enacted

here, when the troopships have sailed home through the Narrows, the great cheers rising from their decks as the Statue of Liberty is passed, the delirious happiness of flags and brass bands upon the quayside; and of all the poignant images of exile this harbor conjures up, the saddest I think is that of the German seamen interned throughout the Second World War in the halls of Ellis Island—only a few hundred yards from the delights of Manhattan, within sight of its magical lights, yet as absolutely isolated there as they would have been on Devil's Island or St. Helena.

But war does not suit New York. Money is this city's business, trade its avocation, creative pleasure its gift, and its philosophies are free-for-all. In such a city war seems only a squalid (if often profitable) distraction: ever since 1815, when the arrival of a British sloop with the news of a peace treaty set the place afire with tumultuous rejoicing, no city in the world has greeted the ending of wars with such unrestrained delight. As it happens America has always won; but in 1969, it seemed to me, New York was so weary of the war in Vietnam, on the other side of the world, that a victory by either side would have been greeted with almost equal relief.

War is unnatural to a great port, dedicated to the exchanges of commerce. I found it difficult to remember that though Russian aircraft maintained a regular service from Moscow to JFK, no Russian ships ever entered the Bay. And nothing seemed more out of character to the Coast Guard, dedicated as they are to the peaceful passage of the world's shipping, than their duties of surveillance over Communist ships in port; for when a Polish vessel comes to New York, a Coast Guard cutter meets it outside the Narrows and escorts it through the Bay. For every moment of its stay in New York, the Coast Guard keep a watch upon it from their loitering launches, until it sails abashed away again, back to the other half.

The indigenous conflicts of New York are frictional, rather than combustible: William James the philosopher wrote of this city's "permanent earthquake condition," but in fact the big eruption seldom comes. It is symptomatic that though the murder rate in this port is ferocious, there have never been race riots on the scale of those in far lesser cities elsewhere in America; the worst riots New York has known were—symptomatic again—those protesting against the draft laws during the Civil War.

Sometimes the perpetual New York skirmish is constructive. One day I went aboard the excursion boat *Miss Circle Line* to see one of the more wholesome city disputes being fought. We were well supplied with drinks and victuals on board; we wore badges with our names upon them; we were sprinkled with celebrities, and armed with waterproofs against the drizzle, and binoculars for the passing sights; we were the Scenic Hudson Preservation Conference, proceeding upstream to protest, in a seminar of speeches and discussions, against the building of a power station at the wrong place.

Many of my fellow passengers looked very familiar. I had met them protesting against the erection of pylons in the Oxfordshire hills, against the demolition of palaces in the back canals of Venice, against copper smelters in Anglesey and Americanization in Alice Springs. They were paisleyed people, head-scarved people, white cardigans over check blouse people, with leather straps worn diagonally across tweedy chests, and speckled bow ties. I even observed an elderly lady wearing a hatpin. They sat in angry concentration in the main saloon, looking at maps and listening to fairly wordy declamations (". . . a meaningful effort to clean up definitively the problem of the river" . . . "finally come up with

an effective realistic mechanism in which we can all meaning-
fully participate . . ."), and when the star of the show, a
presidential candidate of the day, stood up to say his piece,
they received him for the most part, it seemed to me, with
the patronizing indulgence directed towards lesser royalty in
Europe.

Up we chugged through the rain, protesting all the way,
and sometimes peering through the misted windows to see
some Scenic Beauty hideously threatened by, or miraculously
preserved from, progress. Things warmed up as we proceeded.
The presidential candidate left us, being dropped ashore in
Westchester County to a waiting cortege of police cars and
mayoral attentions. The mild and gentlemanly nature of our
disaffection wore thin, we began to say quite rude things
about the Consolidated Edison Company ("If Con Ed could
be boiled down into one man, I wouldn't have him in my
home"), and to my astonishment, at a crucial moment of
the discussion the lady with the hatpin, reaching her hand
into a kind of bird-watcher's reticule made of green canvas,
produced a camera, stood shakily to her feet, and took a
flashlight photograph of us all.

This was a New York conflict of the staidest kind, yet
even so a streak of real bitterness presently began to show.
Nobody was going to forgive and forget. Society in this city
thrives upon abrasion, and politics can be rough. New York
is run by a City Government big enough to rule many a
lesser kingdom, with its Mayor regally in his mansion above
the river (he is one hundred and third in the line of
succession from Thomas Willett, 1665) and its own Ambas-
sadorial office in Washington—a city lobby, so to speak, to
keep the interests of New York in the corporate mind of
Congress. There is a City Council of thirty-eight members,
and an elected President for each of the five boroughs,
providing liaison between the electorate and the various city

departments. The City Government has a larger budget than the State of New York, within whose wider legislative authority this city lies like a monstrous cuckoo in somebody else's nest. Mr. Tobin took me up to Gracie Mansion one morning to meet the Mayor of the day, John Lindsay, and I felt myself to be in the presence not merely of a municipal official, but a Head of State: the formalities were minimal, there were children's paintings on the walls of the Mayor's office, and the Mayor himself struck me as almost too soigné and handsome to be a politician at all; but our conversation ranged across a sweep of subjects fit for any Chancellery, and there were times when I almost called my host Mr. President.

The system of government is intricate to a degree, with its myriad departments and agencies, its Planning Commission and Housing Authority, its Departments of Relocation, and Sanitation, and Correction, and Markets, its Site Selection Board, its Council Against Poverty, even its Board of Ethics. So much bureaucracy might depress the old free enterprisers of the waterfront—the city has its own radio and television station, too. The Official Directory, my favorite New York book, is bound in green and contains more than five hundred pages; its general index begins with the Academy of Music, Brooklyn, and ends with the Zoological Society of Staten Island, its list of names begins with AARNIO, Alpo, and ends with Mary ZWOLENIK (by way of Rufus Youngblood, Ira Toff, Beatrice Shainswit, and Joseph C. Indelicato).

This complexity is compounded by politics, for the city is snarled up with the political in-fighting made notorious long ago by Tammany Hall, and bemused by the hangovers of immemorial political binges. Worse still, the City Government is only one in a whole series of overlapping authorities, often at loggerheads with each other. Within the New York Metropolitan region, as generally defined, there are more than fourteen hundred separate governments, each empowered to raise and spend money. There are town governments, county governments, city governments, State governments, public authorities of several kinds, and a Federal Government over all. "Make Edgewater Great Again," said an election poster I saw one day in one of the infinitesimal townships of the New Jersey shore.

There are the trade unions, too, the great corporations, the public-service bodies, the shipping interests, the railroads, the conservation groups—each with power and influence, each passionately grinding axes. Everybody is up in arms. The State of New York has repeatedly been at odds with the State of New Jersey. In 1804 New York claimed all the land under the Hudson River, bank to bank, so that New Jersey might not build wharves over it; even now, though the State line runs down the middle of the river, New York retains police jurisdiction over "all the waters of the Hudson River" and "over all the lands covered by said waters to the low water mark on the . . . New Jersey side thereof." Both States have laid claim to Staten Island in their time (New York won—the island forms the Borough of Richmond) and it took a pact between the two to decide that whereas the Statue of Liberty is in New York, all the submerged land around Liberty Island is in New Jersey. At one time New Jersey proposed to charge import duty on goods from New York. This dichotomy of the seaport—most of the wharves in New York, most of the railroad terminals in New Jersey— caused trouble for years, and led in the end to the creation of the Port Authority, officially defined to this day as having been founded "by a Compact" between the States.

Then New York City often has squabbles with New York State, and New York State with the Federal Government, and Consolidated Edison with the Hudson Scenic Preservation Council. The estate owners of Long Island protest against new island roads; the developers and builders demand them. The Regional Plan Association argues for more public transport; the car manufacturers predictably disagree. Ornithologists oppose more skyscrapers. The Port Authority demands land for new airports. A savagely specialized controversy was aroused when it was discovered that the erection of the World Trade Center would interfere with television reception not only in Harlem, but also in Westchester County—a problem solved by the Port Authority in best South Street style by transferring all the New York television transmitters from the top of the Empire State to the top of the Trade Center.

And worst of all are the tensions of race—synonymous here, or nearly so, with the tensions of poverty and of envy. New York has become in many ways a laboratory of urban living, a test-bed for us all; but again, though the anxieties it offers are universal, the causes are particular to the city. If these terrible problems seem to dominate the affairs of New York with a particular absoluteness, it is not because black people have been especially badly treated here, or live in worse poverty than elsewhere, but because everything is hotter and more vivid in this forcing-house of humanity.

Somebody described the New York interplay of forces to me as "democracy in a new guise," and it does at least encourage the voicing of opinions. No city talks harder than New York. The result, though, is not the happiness that the Founding Fathers thought it right to pursue. New York has been an ill-governed city for decades; what its apologists call democratic vitality appears to the stranger chiefly as dirt, congestion, ugliness, violence, delay, confusion, and bad temper—the whole perversely illuminated by immense high spirits and great physical beauty. Every public action is delayed by the stubbornness of sectional interests; so it should be, in a democracy, but it must sometimes make the poor citizenry pine, all the same, for an old-school, venal, omnipotent boss.

Take the Verrazano Bridge, which was completed in 1964, and would seem to a visiting commissar, I suppose, a perfectly straightforward solution to a major New York problem. This was at least twenty years in gestation, though only nine in birth. The people of Bay Ridge, Brooklyn, who would be dispossessed by the building of approach roads, fought the project to the bitter end, supported by the powerful Republican machine of Brooklyn; the more determined citizens sat tight in their frame houses when all around them was chaos and destruction, the great troughs of the bulldozers and a haze of dust. Across the Narrows, on the other hand, the politicians of Staten Island fought hard for the bridge, which would end the isolation of the island at last. Across the allegorical gap of the Narrows the opinions vitriolically flew, interest against interest, as though Forts Hamilton and Wadsworth had opened fire upon each other.

Staten Island had acquired an almost symbolic status as a pressure chamber. In its big flat slab of not very interesting country one could see many of the issues clearly at stake, as the forces of change and conservation contended. Separated from Brooklyn by the Narrows, from Manhattan by the Bay, from New Jersey by the meandering waterways of the Kills, its only connections with the mainland were three bridges to New Jersey. It was a long drive around the Bay to Manhattan, via the Hudson tunnels, or half an hour in the ferry (a journey some habitués find so soporific that a friend of mine once forgot he had brought his car on board, walked off at the Battery, and took the subway uptown). Staten Island was isolated from its fellow boroughs in New York City, and remained much the least lively of the five. The oyster communities of its shore had languished with the pollution of the Bay, the farmland of its interior was not very rich, the little townships never seemed to come to much. Attempts to give the community spice or vigor nearly always failed: an opera company, a dog track, a football team, a boxing arena, a baseball team, a symphony orchestra—all fired briefly, and fizzled.

On the other hand in the secluded and deserted alcoves of the island New Yorkers could find, magically preserved at the end of the ferry ride, glimpses of their lost Arcadia: wild flowers in profusion, little wild birds and animals of the foreshore, all the smells of the countryside. Near the beaches were the little clapboard houses of the oystermen, often built by Negroes from the South—some of whom could still be seen, genially lazing away their old age, picturesquely in rocking chairs upon their porches. It was an idyllic place, I gather. Residents of organic tastes much preferred to keep it so, and sophisticated citizens of Manhattan regarded Staten Island as the only remaining link with the old New York, of the green hills and the oyster beds, as it was before mankind broke with the rest of the natural world.

Progress won, of course. The bridge was built; Staten Island was brought within a short easy drive of Brooklyn and Manhattan; and I drove over one day to see how thoroughly the victorious forces had occupied the island. The effect was staggering, so instantly does the momentum of New York sweep in, when once the tangles have been cleared. It was four years since the completion of the bridge, but already the whole feeling and purpose of the island had changed. A huge expressway was being built from one shore to the other, and feeder roads would shortly usher the millions of urban New York into the undeveloped flats, creeks, and marshes of the southern shore. Wherever I drove little square box-houses announced the arrival of the speculators, sign after sign along the country roads—Manors in the Colonial

Style, Colonial Estates, Hi-Art Housing, Durable Homes, Camelot—"Invest in a Stronger America, Invest in a Fine House." Land prices had multiplied already, and the last descendants of the oystermen, now looking distinctly bewildered on their sun-blistered stoops, were clearly in a state of siege.

It was like seeing a blank on the map filled in before your eyes: so many lives altered, so many fortunes made, such traditions shattered and such hopes raised, by the construction of a single lovely bridge.

"Take care!" is a familiar valediction of New York, and with reason: in 1967 there were more murders on the island of Manhattan alone (population 1,900,000) than there were in the whole of England and Wales (population 47 million). It is because the stakes are so high, and the pressures so inexorable, that the atmosphere of New York is so charged with brutality. The moment a ship sails through the Narrows, or a jet touches down at JFK, the demands of this port are felt. "What kind of a name is that?" asked an immigration officer of a new arrival around the turn of the century, eying the signature on the application form. "I'll give you a new name"—but it was his *own* name, Leopold Stokowski replied, and he stuck to it. The standards and values of this seaport, for all its soaring sense of opportunity, impose themselves upon the new arrival. There is little room here for ignorance, or even innocence. The newcomer is expected to know. Time is too short for explanations, and life in New York often proceeds like a very contemporary movie—the cuts are abrupt and often incomprehensible.

All this is, I suppose, because of uncertainty. Emigration is an uncertain business at best, and life in New York is undecided: a new bridge, a new city ordinance, a neighbor of a new color and *wham*—life collapses, and has to be laboriously reconstructed. The violence of New York has spread inland from the waterfront. The shipping business was a fairly cutthroat origin for a city, and South Street was always a violently competitive place: in the old days both pilots and tugmen physically fought each other for business, and no ruse was too dirty for the more ruthless of the clipper captains. Sailing ships made a point of ramming the early steamers, when their hegemony was first threatened. Later the port became a political battleground, with the railroads, the shipping interests, labor, and the politicians all at one another's throats. The Democrats controlled the waterfront, through a network of patronage and bribery; the Republicans controlled the Custom House, and all the jobs and revenues that went with it.

Everybody feels the defensive sourness of New York, and hears its vocabulary on the street: the angry blaring of the horns the moment the lights change, the bitter faces of the drivers—"Get on over, will ya?"—"Will ya look at that bastard?" In the oldest photographs of New York life, taken in the fifties and sixties of the last century, you may already see this acidity creeping in. The immigrants sit in their tenement workshops, sewing dresses, mending shoes, screwing up screws—pinched women in pinafores with sunken cheeks, or heavily bearded Jews wearing their dark hats; and though there is something very moving to these old scenes, and to the hope that brought those people such thousands of miles to this seaport, still one can detect an acrimonious streak already: they look very poor, and hungry, and the rooms they occupy are dark and dingy, and it is impossible to contemplate those old pictures without seeing too the brassy ruthless wealth that lay outside the workshop windows, all the feathered panoplies of Vanderbilts and Rockefellers and the House of Morgan.

Miss Marya Mannes, in her book *The New York I Know,*

dates her disillusionment with a city she greatly loves to the moment when, it seemed to her, the desire for profit finally overtook the nobler human impulses. I think this is an example of that penetrating masochism to which New Yorkers are prone. To me the acrid flavor of New York, which every foreigner notices, comes not from the triumph of a second-rate motive, but from the city's self-knowledge of that triumph. The American adventure remains the grandest, the most beautiful, of all human enterprises; the Declaration of Independence still contains, for my money, the loftiest definition of political purpose; New York, as the gateway of America, has played a more splendid part in history than any other seaport. All this the sensitive New Yorkers know: yet when they look aghast to see what has happened to their city, its waters polluted, its islands degraded, its parks dangerous to walk across, its central streets almost immobile, its blacks and whites, even its Jews and its Negroes, at loggerheads—whenever they fight back, the headlong energy of the place overcomes them again, and tumbles them powerless on.

Many of the most desperate of the New York issues, like those of poverty, housing, and race, are common to most American cities, and many European ones too. The most characteristic of them all is familiar to every city dweller in the Western world, but reaches its apogee in this archipelago. It is congestion. It is a paradigm of the others. It is a kind of ossified motion—the ironic imprint of that universal will to move, "an appetite at any price," that is the basic impulse of New York.

An island narrowness made Manhattan what it is, pushing it upwards, and the wateriness of the archipelago has always forced the New Yorkers huggermugger into confined quarters; but it is the magnetism of the port that has created the astonishing congestion of this place. New York is not merely the greatest business city in the world, it is also the center of the greatest manufacturing complex. Manhattan is only the focus of an enormous urban area, its density of population shading away gradually from the Hudson River, east and west, from nearly 100,000 a square mile in the center, to 10,000 a square mile five miles out, and 100 to the square mile 50 miles out. Before long, pundits say, it will be the vortex of an urban area extending uninterrupted by countryside from Boston in the north to Washington in the south.

The city itself, especially in its poorer parts, is fearfully overcrowded. Worse still, out of this big catchment area a flood of humanity pours through New York each day—in and out of Manhattan in particular, but also from borough to borough, township to township. Sometimes it feels impossible to pack another soul in, as the buses stream in dozen by dozen, as the commuter trains disgorge their thousands into Penn Station and Grand Central, as the Staten Island ferry plods deep-laden across the Bay, and the private cars battle nose to tail through the rush hour into town. New York on a working day seems jammed tight, everything clogged. One summer morning when I was there sixty-two aircraft were lined up on the Kennedy tarmac waiting to take off; flights were delayed for hours, and schedules were affected right across the country to California, so essential is the flow of traffic through this port to the movement of the whole nation.

This violent daily crush most vividly dramatizes the tensions not merely of New York, but of the Western civilization. One cannot escape. There is no solitude, or quiet. "As for privacy," as one nineteenth-century visitor to the city observed, "at any time or under any circumstances, 'tis a thing that enters not into the imagination of America." And if tempers rise among those stuck in traffic jams, living cheek-by-jowl in tenements, or crawling miserably through tunnels, they fly too among those arguing the best ways to cope with it all. Is racial segregation sense or evil? Should they make it easier for cars to enter Manhattan, or harder? Should they encourage the exodus of families to the outer suburbs, or should they defend Manhattan against the fate of many another American city, whose core has been abandoned by the affluent whites, and left to the poor and the colored people? Where can another airport be built? Which should come first, amenity or efficiency? What to do about the black people, or for that matter the white?

The streets of Manhattan, the indicators of all this anxiety, are used during the daytime to their absolute capacity. There is no room for more. The average traffic speed during working hours varies, I am told, from four to six miles an hour, and it takes three times as long to travel twenty blocks now as it did fifty years ago in a horse-drawn carriage. No wonder the nerves of the port are frayed. In the atmosphere of the late 1960s New York often felt to me like a city battened down, all its brilliance, savagery, misery, and brute force precariously held in check. "Who's listening?" asked an advertisement I read one evening, as I lay alone in my apartment, with only the ghostly flicker of my neighbor's television faintly shining through my window. "Are you sure that your home, office, or telephone is not electronically bugged? Be sure that your privacy is protected! Call Sweep Associates today!" I was not at all sure that my privacy was protected, and though I did not in fact call Sweep Associates, I did get up and close the curtains, it suddenly dawning upon me that I was lying within full view of Mr. Huntley and Mr. Brinkley altogether in the nude.

New York is certainly heavily bugged, and laced with closed-circuit television. The doorman at the front door of the apartment building has a television circuit to see what is happening at the back. The policemen at the Bus Terminal have a circuit, to watch events on the street outside. The banks and the tunnels and the department stores have circuits. There was no circuit available on *Miss Circle Line,* when the Scenic Hudson Preservation Conference sailed up-river that day, but I was told that the opposition was sure to have a spy on board instead.

Security checks, fingerprinting, night guards, double locks —these are the stuff of New York. We live in revolutionary times, and in New York everything is more so. In some ways, by European standards, this is a very frank city. Millionaires respond affably to notes from strangers. Tycoons have all the time in the world to talk. The public-relations agencies of Manhattan, where the science of public relations was born, have lost none of their pioneering zeal, but are still ready to grab any likely visitor by the scruff of his neck, thrust a fairly watery Martini into his hand, shower him with pamphlets and call him by incorrect abbreviations of his given name. But behind the glad-handing, I fear, the heart is closed. In Trinity Churchyard, where many a New York worthy lies rotted in vault or catacomb, there is a notice on a gate. "Authorized Personnel Only," it says.

Though all this sets a pace or standard for half the world, it is the norm of New York. It is only a diffuse incidental of portage—from the harbor by way of finance through commerce and the communications industry to an everyday way of life. "Ideal for Retirement," says a sign brightly on a hotel erected immediately beside the noisiest and busiest of the Long Island approach roads, and it is true that New Yorkers have long adapted themselves to the discomforts and incivilities of this city. They do not, it is true, often admit affection for the place. As Irvin S. Cobb once observed of it, it is "the one densely inhabited locality—with the possible exception of Hell—that has absolutely not a trace of local pride." For its native-born citizens, nevertheless, New York is the real thing, and all else is abnormal. When New Yorkers retire, all too often they go to parts of Florida and California where they may be sure of living among other New Yorkers. "I moved out to Staten Island once," an acquaintance told me when I asked if he was not depressed by the tenseness of the city, "but I moved right back again. The silence kept me awake all night."

It is part of life in New York to be insulted, and to be rude back again, in the best waterfront manner. For the most part the discourtesies of New York have no specific application, but are merely an expression of *la condition humaine*. The air rasps with grumble. "Come on, boy," says the stall-keeper to the browsing youth, "you're holding up progress, buy it and get on." "I'm not buying, I'm just looking." "I don't care whether you're buying or looking, you bum," retorts the man, "you're delaying business, move on, will ya?" —and long after the exchange is over, and the youth has sauntered off, he is still mouthing scurrilities to himself, half under his breath, savoring their flavor: "the lousy bum, just looking, the bastard, the cheeky young bum . . ."

He bears no grudge. He has enjoyed the exchange, I think. New Yorkers like salt more than sugar, and do not yearn for *politesse*—just as they have no gift for leisure. They are, rich or poor, black or white, native-born or immigrants, only the children of their harbor, which has lived always by no-holds-barred, and where nothing stays the same.

Chapter 14

THE PASSAGE
CONCLUDED

When Mr. Tobin invited me that day to write this book, he did not I think foresee my passage through his port reaching such metaphysical piers. Nor did I; but over these months I had become absorbed with cause and effect in New York, and what began fifteen chapters back as inquiry, and developed into description, has ended in analysis—self-analysis, perhaps, for one's view of a city is only a mirror-image of oneself.

I had followed as consistent a course as I could, relating what I saw always to the waterfront, and repeatedly pursuing side channels back to their source; but I found that as the subject broadened, from maritime history to social psychology, so my involvement became more and more emotional. "Well," they used to ask at the Port Authority, "what do you make of the place?" But trying to answer such a question was like trying to express a succinct and balanced view on the state of humanity.

Sometimes I thought that none of it was real. The transience of it all, the incessant shift, made it all feel sham, so that the kindness of friends seemed specious, the bonhomie of strangers false. Then the city's naïve respect for appearances depressed me, and its parrot talk, unspeakable snobbery, mock detachment, and reliance upon those most flexible of accessories, statistics. Its sudden swings of taste and fancy, too, expressed in ephemeral cults and art fashions, made me feel that nothing was heartfelt. At other times I was haunted by the pathos of New York. The city seemed to have got out of control, so that its people were merely whisked along by its momentum, impotent to change direction. H. G. Wells had this same sensation in 1906, when he wrote of a "blindly furious energy of growth that must go on . . . the mechanical thing, the unintentional thing which is speeding up all these people, driving them in headlong hurry this way and that." A nervous condition is the condition of New York, and I suspect always has been: the momentum which brought it into being riddles it still, and makes it the archetypical city of an age in which, so prophets suggest, the movement means more than the destination. I was sorry for it: sorry for the obese and horrible little dogs of Manhattan, taken out upon their leads each morning to piss against a tree; sorry for the elderly ladies in Dynel wigs, lunching alone on instant food in hotel restaurants; sorry for all the people, black, white, or brown, caught up in the passions or history and instinct; sorry above all for the idea of the place, which is marvelous beyond compare, but has gone sour.

But then again there was the elixir of it! Nowhere else has the lyrical exuberance of New York, when the mood and morning is right, and the ships are astir in the great Bay, and all is life and enterprise. Then I forgot the squalors of this civilization, and remembered only the glories, and thought of all the gifted people the city was inspiring all about me: the actors, the writers, the artists, the dancers, the designers, the architects, the musicians, who have translated the gusto of an old seaport into so many un-nautical marvels. It so happened that at the very end of my work in New York the last of the great transatlantic liners made her maiden entrance into the port—the last of the really big ones, that is, in the old tradition of swank and superlatives. The *Queen Elizabeth 2* is as much a work of art as of engineering, deliberately intended as a glittering display-house of decorative skills and innovations. Rumors of her discotheque décor had upset those many New Yorkers who associate the British maritime tradition with mahogany paneling and seagoing butlers, but I liked the sound of her. She was something new in ships, she had reached 32 knots on trials, and she was in a sense my property, in that with my fellow taxpayers I had advanced £25 million towards her cost; so all in all I thought her appearance in the upper bay would provide a fine celebratory conclusion to my passage through New York.

In a way I was right, for it turned out to be a wonderfully happy occasion, and made me feel I had been properly initiated into the mysteries of the harbor. I went out to meet the *QE2* on one of the McAllister tugs, sailing from the Battery. The McAllisters are an old New York family of tug and harbor men, Irish by origin, ebullient by disposition, and hospitable. Three of their boats sailed that morning in close formation, and they were loaded down with what seemed to me to be several hundred McAllisters— grave elder McAllisters, gay miniskirted McAllisters, gossipy McAllister matrons, virile McAllister bravos. The boats themselves were naturally named for McAllister ladies, and on their decks, rather loosely kitted out in green kilts and tam-o'-shanters, the pipers of the New York Donegal Pipe Band played in lusty antiphony across the waves. There was a satisfying buffet lunch on board, and plenty to drink, and by the time we had passed beneath the Verrazano Bridge, and saw the elegant and spindly outline of the *QE2* approaching from the open sea, I felt myself an honorary McAllister for the day, and looked out across the water with a Donegal benevolence.

The harbor is the most beautiful of New York's possessions, and nowadays it is one of the last refuges in an unhappy metropolis of that fizz and crackle, that sense of lovers' release, which once used to be synonymous with Manhattan. Here some of the American pageantry survives, and when the *QE2* sailed in that day much of the old American generosity showed too, and the sense of fun, and the sentimental loyalty. The sea was choppy and the wind rough, but the sun came out just as the ship passed through the Narrows, and so in a bright flurry of flags and foam our procession passed through the Bay. The liner towered above us high, bright and very new, almost fragile. The sky was thick with helicopters and seaplanes, idling happily about there like kites, or paper airplanes, and all around us scores of little ships noisily and exuberantly escorted the liner towards her berth.

On the forecastle of the *Queen* the ships' cooks, in their chefs' hats, gazed impassively towards Manhattan, and in an open door in the flank of the liner a solitary white-clad sailor stood silhouetted nonchalant, even bored, against the black inside, as though such spectacles were observable on every voyage. For the rest, everybody seemed to be waving. We waved, all barriers down, at total strangers. We blew kisses all over the place. A girl in a blue dress jumped up and down with excitement on the boat deck, and through the slightly steamy windows of what I took to be some ferociously air-conditioned or centrally heated lounge, I could see pale elderly faces cautiously peering into the open air outside, looking wistfully nostalgic still, I fancied, for mahogany and Palm Court.

What fun it all was! The sirens constantly blew. The flags

fluttered from every mast. The Staten Island ferry chugged by with a huge welcome sign hanging from its superstructure. The aircraft buzzed. The Donegal pipers, temporarily abandoning their reels and coming disarmingly apart at the joints of their accouterments, were to be encountered in odd corners of the tugboats merrily drinking Scotch and swapping badinage. Now and then waves of water sloshed through the scuppers of our boat, washed the legs of the buffet table, and made us all leap onto deck chairs; but nobody much minded, the best came out in all of us, the world was fine, New York was laughing, and as the noble ship paced up the Hudson River and turned into her berth, news came over the tug's radio that Mrs. Gerard McAllister, my hostess, had just become a grandmother.

I remembered, as we limped damply but contentedly ashore that afternoon, looking all those months before at my photograph of the Bay, and presumptuously claiming it to be mine. Now, I thought, it really was. No Briton alive, I am sure, had seen more of New York harbor, or knew it better, or felt more at home upon its wide, dirty, magical waters.

I wish I could end there, but it would be an evasion. In my book as in life, the port has become The City. For all the space and glory of the harbor, it is here that an increasingly urban man has reached his vexed fruition, and it would be wrong to end such an account with a scene of festival. At this moment of its history New York is scarcely a festive place. It is in some ways the most majestic city I know, and in some respects the most beautiful, but its people seem to be the least contented. To Henry James, at least in some of his moods, the momentum of New York was its chief horror— "all the sounds and silences, grim, pushing, trudging silences too, of the universal will to move." In 1913 the painter John Marin, one of the first American modernists, painted a picture called *Movement, 5th Avenue,* in which the city itself seemed to be seized by movement, tumbling and piled up by movement, a clock half toppled, buildings apparently cracking, the street seething with indistinguishable hastening traffic.

To me this capture of instrument by function was the true discovery of my passage through New York. This city is not, of course, a sham at all—its power, its art, its wealth are all too real; but it is illusory, in that it is always provisional, never finished or satisfied. It is a commodity of its own port. I suppose there is no human artifact that greets you more absolutely than Manhattan, as your ship swings through the Narrows into the Bay, or your helicopter scuds past Tompkinsville. Grand and uncompromising the skyscrapers stand there, in a miasma of movement around their feet, windows flashing in the sunshine, aerials prodding the sky, radars twirling, jets streaking this way and that. At first I had seen this incomparable spectacle as an exclamation mark, a shout of triumph from the New World. Later it seemed to me an interrogative—where are we bound for? Is our course right?

And so in the end I was left, like so many voyagers before me, trapped by the great port. I loathed it like a lover. The questions it asked I resented; the answers it gave I mistrusted; the spell of it, the chivvying of conscience, the temptations, the delight, I felt to be unfair. Damn you, New York! Damn the bright sweep of your spaces, and the ungainly poetry of your names! A curse on all your archipelago, and on those rough fresh winds off your Bay—which, catching me like an embrace as I stepped out of the helicopter, so often ravished my spirits, and made my heart sing!

REFUNDS

I am in debt to the many New Yorkers who advanced me the wherewithal for this voyage, especially those who so kindly explained particular aspects of the port, or corrected my statistics (which I generally made up as I went along), or showed me around the harbor, or allowed me to poke about their premises, or eavesdrop. I hope they will accept for themselves the compliments of the book, and skip the aspersions.

I am indebted too to a number of other books which I have repeatedly consulted or cribbed from. Among general works I must mention I. N. P. Stokes' *The Iconography of Manhattan Island* (six volumes, 1915–28); *The Epic of New York City*, by Edward Robb Ellis (1966); *The New York I Know*, by Marya Mannes (1961); *New York Proclaimed*, by V. S. Pritchett and Evelyn Hofer (1964); *A Natural History of New York City*, by John Kieran (1959); Bayrd Still's compilation *Mirror for Gotham* (1956); and the splendidly handy Michelin *Guide to New York City* (1968). Books more specific to my subject include *The Rise of New York Port*, by R. G. Albion (1939); *The Bottom of the Harbor*, by Joseph Mitchell (1959); and *The Bridge*, by Gay

Talese (1964). I am grateful for the help of the New York Public Library and the library of the Port of New York Authority, and for the wise advice as always of my New York agent, Julian Bach.

Pictures 1–6, 8, 10, 13, 15, 17, 19–21 are printed by courtesy of the Port of New York Authority. Picture 12 is printed by courtesy of the Moran Towing & Transportation Co., Inc.

Finally my thanks, affection, and apologies to Mr. Daniel Kurshan, a New Yorker often indignant at my views, but a man for a' that.